# The Managerial Ideas from the East

Copyright © 2012 by Yoshifumi Taguchi

The Managerial Ideas from the East
Published by Babel Press U.S.A.
All rights reserved.

No part of this book may be used, reproduced, stored in a retrieval system, or transmitted, in any from or by any means, electric, mechanical, photocopying, recording, or otherwise, without the prior written permission of the author except in the case of brief quotations embodies in critical articles and reviews.

This book was originally published in Japanese under the title
" 東洋からの経営発想 "
by Yu - Un - Sha, Tokyo, Japan in 2010.

Translation in English by Yumi Noji
Supervision of Translation by Peter M. Skaer
Stylish editing by Yuko Yoshida
Cover design by Yuko Yoshida

ISBN - 13: 978-0983640257
ISBN - 10: 0983640254

Babel Corporation
Pacific Business News Bldg. #208,
1833 Kalakaua Avenue,
Honolulu, Hawaii 96815

Phone: (808) 946 - 3773
Fax: (808) 946 - 3993

Website: www.bookandright.com

# The Managerial Ideas from the East

## 「東洋からの経営発想」

Yoshifumi Taguchi

BABEL Press U.S.A.

# Contents

**Preface**
Respecting the Lives of Others — vii

**Chapter 1: What Corporations Are** — 1
1. Why We Were Born — 1
2. The Value of Life — 4
3. The Expression of the Vitality and Happiness of Life — 7
4. The Work Ethic — 9
5. The Sociality of Business — 14

**Chapter 2: Exploring Management Approaches of the East** — 21
1. The Meaning of "Akemashite" — 21
2. Kurōto Cultivation Program — 24
3. Overcoming Dualism — 26
4. "Goodness Is Like Water" in Action — 28
5. Learning Product Planning from ZeamiPreface
   Respecting the Lives of Others — 30
6. Sun Tzu: The Origin of Strategy — 33
7. Leading a Fulfilled Life — 36
8. The Essence of Corporate Social Responsibility — 38
9. The Teachings of Taoism — 41
10. Learning Creativity from Matsuo Bashō — 44
11. Learning Work Ethics from Sen no Rikyū — 47
12. Learning Sales Strategies from Musashi Miyamoto — 49
13. An Invitation to Infinite Thinking — 52
14. Human Potential is the Key to Success — 54

| | | |
|---|---|---|
| 15. | In-en-ka: The Fundamentals of Personal Relationships | 57 |
| 16. | Co-Creation and Coexistence  The 21st Century Business Model | 59 |
| 17. | Learning Work Ethics from Shōsan Suzuki | 62 |
| 18. | Management Based on  "Self-Benefit for the Benefit of Others" | 65 |
| 19. | A New Model for Corporations according to  Hōnen Shonin | 68 |
| 20. | Learning a Customer  Driven Business Practice from Zen | 70 |
| 21. | Transforming Business with Taoism | 73 |
| 22. | Learning Employee  Company Relationships from Dōgen Zenji | 75 |
| 23. | The Essence of Leadership | 78 |
| 24. | The Synthesis of Eastern and Western Wisdom | 80 |

**Afterword** 84

# Preface

**RESPECTING THE LIVES OF OTHERS**

What could be more important than "respect for life" ? It is very important to think candidly about this question. Because, I believe, a new enterprise should start from the belief that nothing comes above the preciousness of being alive. This is the foundation of the view of corporate philosophy based on theories of life. Roughly divided, there are three main points to consider for this idea of "respect for life" which should be adopted by businesses or incorporated into the business management theory as their theme. They are:

1. Why we were born;
2. The value of life; and
3. The expression of the vitality and happiness of life.

Needless to say, these self-inquiries must be relevant to the nature of corporate management. The purpose of businesses is to offer value to society or people's lives and their livelihood. What makes businesses unique is that they can be called for accountability of their fulfillment. And, since their existence relies on the exchange between the value they offer and the value and price society and customers agree to give to the businesses in return, these points have to be relevant to this exchange. This is where a business differs from a government agency or nonprofit organization.

Another important thing to keep in mind is a point of view that is essential for examining the theories of enterprises and business management: "Global universality and the originality cultivated from native soil and climate." The leading technologies such as the internet have prompted many businesses to globalize. Therefore, it is no surprise that people look to businesses for universality that goes beyond ethnicity, tradition and history. And it is quite apparent from the current state of the affairs of multinational enterprises how crucial the business management that embodies the needs of the times is when contemplating effective management. Businesses around the world are coming to embrace these two points:

1. Strengthen the corporation's social significance
2. Establish the attitude toward work based on human nature

That means the new business philosophy has to have the elements that reinforce these two points.

But at the same time, what is equally important is the effectiveness in which businesses utilize their valuable assets – the unique and original culture that was born out of the local soil and climate and has been cultivated over time. Having been defeated in World War II, Japan experienced a time in which its people flatly denied any Japaneseness. They had turned to the victor, the United States, for anything they thought to be first-class and superior. Combined with the national character, a devotion to anything American seems to have become too excessive. I think Japan should take this moment, even however brief, to reflect on its culture which is rooted deeply in its own soil and climate and reassess its excellence.

The influence the soil and climate have on us is immeasurable. For instance, if one tries to live on the southern island with the lifestyle long fostered in the northern regions, discord will arise naturally. If such disparity occurs even within modestly sized Japan, we can see how it is quite unreasonable for the people who grew up in Japan, with the soil and climate of the East, to try modeling themselves after the corporate culture of America that has been fostered in its local Western surroundings. To Western eyes, such attempts to adapt may seem rather an awkward and poor imitation. And well-educated and cultured Westerners would certainly say: "Why do people in Japan not appreciate their own highly-developed and rich traditional spiritual culture, which the West does not even come close to?" To people from the West, this must appear rather awkward. Awkwardness causes strain and eventually strain will lead to collapse.

As long as a company did businesses only in Japan, therefore serving only the fellow Japanese, Americanized mimicry may have pleased its customers. But as the effects of globalization sweeps through, forcing businesses to expand its market worldwide, they will be surrounded by the Western competitors. As a business's success hinges increasingly on authenticity, Japanese businesses have to have "something with a Japanese-exclusive edge." Furthermore, this unique "Japaneseness" could be quite effective in the direction businesses around the world are headed to. And Japanese wisdom rooted in its long tradition should definitely be incorporated by global enterprises.

When seeking Japaneseness, the first thing that comes to mind is the idea of "respect for life." At the very root of Japan's traditional spiritual culture, this distinctive perspective on life is firmly embedded. This regard for life is, I believe, what the twenty-first-century Japanese enterprises need to firmly adhere to as their foundation.

Now, let us contemplate on the first part of this book:

1. Why We Were Born
2. The Value of Life
3. The Expression of the Vitality and Happiness of Life
4. The Work Ethic
5. The Social Role of Business

# Chapter 1

# What Corporations Are

## 1-1 WHY WE WERE BORN

The Doctrine of the Mean, one of the classic Chinese texts in the Four Books and Five Classics, begins with this expression: "The order of heaven is called nature." We could have been born as anything – dog, cat, tree, flower and so on – but we were born as a human. This, it says, is exactly in accordance with the order of heaven. Therefore, each of us needs to realize the fact that we were born as a human indicates we are already entrusted with a special mission. This mission is to live our life in conformity with our nature, to live as a human.

To live as a human is to live our life through fully exerting our human nature. Human nature is the quality unique to us that no other animals share. It is simply what makes human a human. It encompasses mind, awareness and soul. All of which are considered to exist separate from the body, but pertain to mental aspects and activities. That means what is distinctive to a human is the spiritual nature and mental activities. And to heighten and deepen these aspects are the responsibilities those who came to this world as humans have to fulfill. What arises from this spiritual nature can also be defined as human nature.

In classic Chinese texts, human nature is expressed in "go-jyō," or the five elements – benevolence, righteousness, ritual, wisdom and integrity. Benevolence signifies the love for all mankind. In terms of relationships in real society, benevolence represents happiness one wishes for family members and society. Righteousness refers to orderly acts and self-devotion to the common good while putting aside one's own interests. Righteousness also means to fulfill one's given role wholeheartedly. Ritual portrays the set of standards descended from the order of the universe which people should have in order to maintain the social order. Wisdom expounds judgment and knowledge granted only to humankind and discretion one exercises. Integrity means to be devoid of lies, deceit and dishonesty.

Companies are a part of human society and composed of a group of people. Given this fact, companies need to be a place, first and foremost, where people can cultivate and deepen their spiritual nature and where workers can freely exert their human natures. In addition, the value companies create has to be the manifestation of these spiritual and human natures. The meaning of our existence is to express and cultivate our spiritual and human nature. Therefore, if this idea is absent from the foundation of corporate activities, what businesses do become quite contrary to the underlying principle of the nature described in the Doctrine of the Mean. Given the present state, unless businesses change their ways, corporate scandals will persist and worse, businesses will never earn the respect of society.

The major league baseball player Ichiro Suzuki has brought a spiritual nature of virtuosity into the game of baseball. He has been successfully establishing the advantages of mental training on the pragmatic American soil. The direction of businesses should also be set in this realm where their performance is driven by deeper spiritual and human nature. Otherwise, they will have to accept unfavorable receptions by society and be compelled to endure the perception that they inhibit human nature while finding no prospect nor hope in their future.

A human activity in human society is, in essence, about progress and advancement.

Therefore, one needs to keep in mind that perceiving businesses as mere means of making money only hurts oneself. Besides, such thinking is not for the wise.

The human nature described in the Doctrine of the Mean demands each of us to be aware of our innate mission as a human. It holds much deeper meaning than simply having been given a life in this world. For us humans, the universal theme is how we can heighten our minds and fully exert our human nature. We are at a point where the same theme needs to be seriously considered for business environments.

"Have companies matured?" This has been a long-time proposition of mine. Are there any business organizations that could measure up to the outstanding and distinctive group of people such as an orchestra, a soccer team, or a film production company led by legendary directors Kurosawa or Ozu? If the answer is no, why is this so? Perhaps a more relevant question to ask is: "How can we create a corporation that exceeds such highly-respected and excellent teams of individuals?" Of course, the world has its share of inexperienced and less-than-ideal achievers. What we need to focus on is how to raise the level to a higher tier. First, an important point is whether the products or services companies offer continuously demand greater spiritual and human nature. Even for a single commodity, daily pursuit to better spiritual and human nature is essential. The imperturbable desire for truth that allows no room for hurried compromise becomes central. For services, it is about striving to offer quality that could surpass the ultimate spirit of chanoyu, or tea ceremony – superb quality of hospitality so magnificent and filled with excitement and awareness that it transforms the customer's expectations.

All of this may seem like veering into spirituality territory, but essentially, it entirely depends on whether we can overcome the contradiction between the individual and the whole. It is not about choosing either the individual or the whole. It is about selecting both the individual and the whole and elevating them to what the Japanese philosopher Kitaro Nishida once said: "Self-identity of the absolute contradiction." Basically, it is about whether the state of the whole, where the ability of the individual is heightened, and the state of each individual, where organizational strength of the whole is heightened, align with the concept of the ancient Chinese philosophy Yin and Yang: "Binding the opposites together to create a greater whole."

What this means is that we need to understand the best situation for both the individual and the whole. And what we can do is first strengthen the organizational theory based on an autonomous decentralization system and their complementary relations, then establish the optimal situation with a careful comprehensive vision that grasps the greater whole.

What each employee needs to do is strengthen his or her self-disciplined excellence based on the individual work ethic. What companies need to do is to guard and enhance the activities of the employees with their brand recognition and public confidence. Recognition and confidence are established through companies' accumulation of tradition and achievements, as well as their capacity for information gathering, processing and communication. Companies also need to create an exciting work environment that encourages free flow of creativity for their employees. At the foundation of these efforts we see the firmly held devotion to the elevation of our spiritual and human nature.

## 1-2 THE VALUE OF LIFE

Eiichi Shibusawa, the late Japanese industrialist, once said: "Commerce is not commerce without morality. Morality is not morality without commerce." "Morality" here can be interpreted as a sense of ethics people have that is beyond the rule of law. It is a criterion of judgment for determining whether something is too unconscionable to sympathize with as humans even though laws may permit it.

Laws are created by people; therefore, they are subject to revisions and transformations at anytime. On the other hand, a traditional sense of ethics long cultivated in the local soil and climate, rarely wavers. The morality Shibusawa refers to is this kind of ethicality. He says regardless of its legality, if something appears distrustful or suspicious to many, it should not be done. Shibusawa felt the need to interject moral obligation because commerce is directly and indirectly ingrained into human desire.

Controlling human desire is incredibly challenging, but it has to be done, especially under business circumstances. Desire knows no boundary, and self-control often comes short. Desire is like a very sharp knife: it could slit the hand of the holder, or worse, cut other people.  The primary objective of commerce is to increase wealth, while the primary objective of businesses is to expand its operation. Ambition fuels the efforts toward expanding wealth, and ambition originates in none other than desire. Desire should not be denied because without it we would see neither improvements nor progress in our society. But there is a limit to how much we can control it. And because of its inherent nature, it only gets bigger, eventually exceeding its limits. Once the threshold is crossed, self-control no longer functions. As a result, we, who are supposed to be in charge of keeping it under control, become slaves to it. At that point, we are extremely shortsighted, even blind to our surroundings and society, and are completely absorbed in enlarging desire.

Originally, business was supposed to be conducted for the purpose of supporting the happiness and well-being of society and customers. And that is why companies are rewarded by their customers with their sympathy and resonances, support and endorsement, affinity and patronage – all of which enable them to grow and expand. But because it is the nature of desire to completely upset such rationale, if consumed by desire, businesses will eventually neglect and disregard society and their customers. And this could even escalate into the deception and deprivation of the lives of others.

The basic principle of morality is, first of all, to fully understand and master 'the way,' or the Tao – the originator of the universe. The basis of this pursuit is called "virtue." A quote from the opening of the Doctrine of the Mean mentioned earlier – "the order of heaven is called nature" – is followed by "to follow nature is called the way. To pursue the way is called learning." To live a life never forgetting or losing sight of the meaning of having been given a life as a human is to live in accordance with the way, or the Tao. And to strive to be someone who is determined never to stray from the path is learning. If it is in one's nature to constantly exert oneself to elevate one's own spirituality, and if the basic human nature of benevolence, righteousness, ritual, wisdom and integrity firmly exist at one's core, it is hard to imagine such an individual would be overcome by desire and do something like disregarding the lives of others.

Nature is a concept which embodies, quite obviously, life. That means, above all things, life must be respected. I wonder if this idea conforms to the primary objective of corporate activity – profitability. First of all, corporate profitability cannot be sustained without the relationship based on a mutual trust with society. In other words, profitability depends on whether a company can build a stronger and more long-term personal relationship with its customers, and how it can establish such relationships with as many customers as possible. The foundation of personal relationships is to have respect for each other's lives. Never go too far as to take the lives of others – this has been a fundamental human belief that we should have. It is because once a life is taken, every aspect of a reciprocal relationship is over. Even if one is engaged in a fight, one always find a way to enjoy oneself and the fight itself. This is called being cultured, and it was thought that loss of a life means the end of pleasure. That is why when swordsmen of the highest rank fight, they may deliver cuts, but only skin deep, nothing further. Or, they may strike the opponent with the back of the sword instead.

The nature mentioned earlier is a part of one's life. Therefore, if one has a profound sense of gratitude toward the fate of having been born, especially as a human, one would respect the lives of others as much as one respects one's own life, knowing other people lead their lives in the same way.

In the East, especially Japan, a belief in respecting not just fellow humans' but also the lives of all living things, all creations on the earth, has endured. "Sō-moku-koku-do-shikkai-jōbutsu": Everything in this world – plants, trees, earth – though they may bear no soul, they will all attain Buddhahood. Yet, humans consume living things. We, in other words, continue to survive while taking the lives of others. Our sustainability depends on other lives. How should we deal with such a contradiction? The concept of "ekō," or "merit transference," provides an answer.

Originally, it comes from praying for departed souls by offering a good deed, namely "seigan," or a "vow." It was a hope for the salvation of all living things. Later, it became a hope for all things that lost their lives to attain eternal Buddhahood. It then evolved into a gratitude for the animals or fish that we sacrifice and an attitude of not being wasteful and making the most of what we have sacrificed. There is deep gratitude for all living things that have died to nourish and sustain each of our lives.

When carried over to the work environment, such an attitude becomes a mindset toward handling materials and tools with utmost care. In the field of carpentry, carpenters say they "read the mind of wood." They carefully examine every single piece of wood they work with to determine the most suitable application. They even pay attention to the environment of where trees have grown. For example, they avoid using hardwood which grew on the frigid north side of a mountain on the north side of a house. Without this practice, "mismatched wood" is said to compromise, after awhile, the frame alignment of the house.

Reading the minds of materials, utilizing them with the highest efficiency and making an effort to keep waste to the absolute minimum – even today these ideas are carefully considered among the manufacturing sector of the leading-edge industries. Apparently, the same traditions and practices are being carried on.

Each and every material once had a life of its own. An effort to bring out the most of its original vitality means to maximize the use of the material without any waste. It is a mindset that believes seemingly lifeless material is going to renew itself through a new application. Needless to say, behind it is the mind that appreciates, values and respects all lives.

## 1-3 THE EXPRESSION OF THE VITALITY AND HAPPINESS OF LIFE

*V*itality is the power to live and the capacity for survival. The exuberant vigor and actions are arguably the origin of humans. The intensity and drive that radiate from people who are engaging in or have accomplished something is none other than vitality.

A company is a group of people united with a common goal to offer values to society. It is a place that tries to accomplish something. This means that what is absolutely necessary for a business enterprise is vitality. Therefore, before focusing on its activities, a company should really examine and consider passionately how it can be a place where vitality is sustained and expressed. It could even ask itself why it lacks vitality.

There are what a company has to think about and what the people who work for it have to think about. We must clarify them first. What a company needs to consider is how to provide its employees an environment that inspire them to exert their vitality spontaneously. It is a company's responsibility to make such a workplace available to its workers. I mention this because there are too many workplaces that can only be seen as a place where vitality diminishes. The word "management" itself seems to promote this to take place. When it comes to managing workers, it is often about how to confine them in a certain box and keep them from stepping out. Therefore, the company is generally dismissive of the actions of its workers.

What happens if people are always denied? They will become the embodiment of self-restraint and stop acting freely and lively with their arms and legs outstretched. Over time, they will become complacent with such confinement and become insensible to pain. They may even find themselves comfortable in such an environment. There is such a thing as pleasure in not stepping out, not going outside the box, or not stretching out. As they continue to suppress their vitality, they eventually forget what vibrancy of life was, and think what is best for them are tranquil and ordinary days that are free of problems.

Since such companies which suppress vitality are needless to say unfit for the turbulent turning point businesses are in today, they will be forced to make drastic changes. Once a piece of rubber shrinks and hardens, it is impossible to restore it to be soft and elastic again. Therefore, businesses have to have clear and firm ideas about how they and their workplaces should be.

When our vitality is fully exerted, our spirit becomes enriched. What, then, do we need to do to enrich our spirit? To start, here is what companies need to consider. In the morning when, let's say, Mr. Yamada and Ms. Tanaka arrive at work, a company should acknowledge that is it actually the spirit of Mr. Yamada and Ms. Tanaka that have arrived. In other words, businesses need to recognize spirit and be mindful of how they can satisfy it.

The happiness of being alive arises from a desire. But how can one harbor an ardent desire as such that one cannot wait to show up to work, day after day? Anticipation of receiving praise, being assigned to exciting projects, having someone to look forward to seeing – it is by knowing what makes one's spirit happy are waiting at the workplace. To receive praise and be highly regarded, respected and counted on by the company, and also to have something stimulating, interesting, engaging and absorbing at one's place of work – all of these bring joy to the spirit. What companies need to do first and foremost is to offer an environment where such elements always await workers.

Also, it is said that our spirit is most fulfilled when it is fully expressing itself. Some have even said that our spirit experiences the greatest gratification when it is truly resonated and united with the others' spirits. That means a place that allows us to openly express ourselves and resonate and unite with the others is actually a place where we collaborate and co-create with other people. This is what a workplace needs to be. It is the same idea as to why we find singing or playing music with the others so joyous, or playing group games so enjoyable. The workplace as a place of collaboration and co-creation – these seem to be the key words. And what follows after that is equally important. Making sure that workers feel a sense of accomplishment after reaching goals or satisfaction of receiving praise by giving them due recognition that will motivate and encourage them for new challenges – having such mechanisms in place is also definitely vital.

## 1-4 THE WORK ETHIC

The intensity of their workers' vitality becomes the intensity of companies' vitality. This energy is the very nature of companies' organizational capabilities. The classic treatise The Art of War has a passage: "A skillful tactician is likened to the sotsuzen. The sotsuzen is a snake that lives in the mountain called Jōsan. If you strike the snake's head, you will be attacked by its tail; if you strike its tail, you will be attacked by its head. If you strike its middle, you will be attacked by both its head and tail. Handling someone with such persistence is no easy task. One cannot be called a topflight soldier unless one has this level of tenacity." This passage describes what vitality is. Vitality is the determination to survive no matter what. Imagine how powerful a company would be if every worker was brimming with such vigor.

Above all else, companies have to be a place where such individuals gather, because it is the workers themselves who enjoy such an environment the most. It is the workers themselves who have the most pleasure from their improving skills and achieving excellence.

The most exciting environment for them is where they can fully exert their skills and abilities. They may encounter strong pressures, but a professional has to be able to enjoy every situation in spite of its challenges. This is what I find very problematic for today's businesses.

It is quite surprising how many of the working people are unsure of why they work.

Why do we work – because it is not made clear to many for one reason or another, and we cannot explain it with conviction, we continue to be unsatisfied with why we have to work. A lot of people have entered the workforce with very passive motives such as social conventions, graduating from college, or reaching a certain age. The fact that they do not yet know what they really want to do means they have settled for the current job halfheartedly while still hoping for more time to think about where they want to be. They would rather continue to live off their parents – the mindsets that contribute to the steady increase of NEETs, people currently "not in education, employment, or training."

What led them to this mindset could only be explained by the waning of the traditional work ethics, which was also the foundation of Japanese society. Having ideal work ethics does not directly motivate people to seek employment; however, there was a time when the society as a whole shared an expectation that adults work, while young people study as they impatiently await the day they could join the adults. Moreover, at that time men had spent their youth anticipating the day they become a father, and women a mother. Today such family values are, too, very sparse. First and foremost, we have to adamantly restore Japan's traditional work ethics.

When it comes to Japan's traditional work ethics, the words of Sen no Rikyū, the renowned master of chanoyu, or the Japanese tea ceremony, capture it all: "Practice and master what you do as if they were the Buddhist practices." When asked of the essence of chanoyu, particularly the wabi-cha style of tea ceremony Rikyū had established, he said: "It is to attain the way and reach enlightenment through practicing with devotion to Buddhism." An attainment of the way, or the Tao, is the fundamental principle of Japan's traditional work ethics. To attain the way, or the Tao, is to acquire the teachings of the Tao, thus reaching enlightenment. In other words, people used to think the purpose of their work was to attain enlightenment.

One day, with a strong desire to be enlightened, Jukō Murata, the founder of wabi-cha and a teacher of Rikyū, entreated a Zen Buddhist priest Ikkyū to take him in to practice Zen meditation at his temple. But Ikkyū bellowed out at Murata, "The teachings of Buddhism lies in the practice of chanoyu!" He told Murata that the path to enlightenment can be found in Murata's own professional activity; therefore, he should perform chanoyu as if practicing Buddhism.

It appears that this spirit was carried on by Rikyū. He also said one's job provides the place and opportunities for Buddhist training. To put it in another way, no matter what we do for work, if all we do is to merely perform tasks, we cannot expect to achieve much in life. It is important to engage in our work as if it is a means to attain enlightenment. It does not matter if we are a businessperson, a baseball player, a cab driver, or a homemaker. We need to carry out our duty as if it is a practice – a practice to attain enlightenment.

That means we can also say that work is a process to reach enlightenment, or the way. This idea transformed jujitsu, the classical Japanese martial art, causing it to evolve into jūdō, or the gentle way, and the arrangement of flowers to kadō, the way of flowers. It further expanded into ideas, such as "the way of businessperson" and "the way of baseball," to turn everything one does into a means to attain the way. This attitude, then, led to the establishment of work ethics where people engage in their work in pursuit of enlightenment.

Japanese are often perceived as turning everything into 'the way.' But this idea is the manifestation of the people's desire to reach a higher spiritual ground. It is a rather recent phenomenon to consider one's work as a way to merely consume and accumulate wealth. Before the shift, people of Japan treated their work as training tools and opportunities, putting less emphasis on the outcome of their labors. Even today, those who have reached the highest level of mastery in their fields are designated and honored as "Living National Treasures."

Considering one's work as a process to reach enlightenment and calling what one does "the way of ···" originated not only in Buddhism but was equally influenced by the classic Chinese philosophies of Confucianism and Taoism. These classics called the origin of the universe the Tao, or the way. The Tao gave birth to all existence. As a matter of fact, it continues to create myriads of things today. The creation and evolution of all existence originates from the workings of the Tao. The essence of the Tao is creation. Creation takes place unceasingly in the entire universe. But the Tao does not just create things. It creates things that are rather dynamic, energetic and even organic because all things share the same origin.   An act of learning, acquiring and making what one learned as a part of oneself by following the nature of the way, or the Tao, is called "virtue." Combining the two – the way and the virtue – we have "the way of virtue." This is the basic principle of morality. Morality is often perceived as ethics, but this is not entirely the case. The way does not create things on impulse or incoherently. It looks at the whole so it can maintain the "order." Morality is about not disrupting this order of the whole, and this concept is the foundation of ethics.

People favor, respect and emphasize the way, or the Tao, through the traditional work ethics because to follow and emulate the essence of the Tao – the origin of the universe, which ensures the stabilization and perpetual existence of the world – is the order of the world, the path to enlightenment.

Similar to other traditional spiritual cultures in Japan, this approach toward work was passed down by the ancestors who were greatly influenced by Confucianism, Buddhism and Taoism. Their unique ideas were well incorporated into their work and motivations to labor. Some may wonder whether Japan's own Shinto religion had an influence over these work ethics. It, too, contributed significantly. The most notable idea is the worship of Inari, one of the principal deities of Shinto.

The numbers of shrines dedicated to the deity of Inari shows how influential and wide spread its worship was in Japan. There are many shrines dedicated to various deities in the country, but the Inari shrines are said to be by far the most numerous. The Chinese characters for Inari have changed over time, so the character used today derives from ine-nari, the cultivation of rice. Although there are different anecdotes as to why it had evolved into Inari, the deity of Inari originated from a deity who carried a sheaf of rice on its shoulder. The old depictions often show the deity shouldering a sheaf of rice on both ends of a pole.

The foundation of the Inari worship is the idea of "cooperation between the deity and people." It was believed that growing rice was not something farmers took on by themselves. It was considered to be an activity which farmers engaged in together with the deity. Specifically, it was believed that the deity "entrusted" the farmers with the cultivation of rice. To entrust means to designate others to carry out the responsibility on one's behalf, therefore, the deity had charged the farmers with rice production on its behalf. That meant farming was an act where the people and the deity became one. Since rice fields were thought to be where the connection between the deity and farmers occurred, they had to be kept in proper condition at all times. No disorder or impurity was tolerated. In this sense, rice fields were considered as very sacred grounds.

Through the labor of cultivation, farmers felt the presence of the deity, conversed with it and believed in the power of the divine. They pushed themselves a little harder so that the deity would willingly offer its hand. There was no need to travel to a shrine or to a designated sacred place. All farmers needed to do was to go to their fields. To them nothing was more sacred than their fields. They knew their fields were exactly where they could meet the deity.

As expressed in the phrase "an act of god," good rice grows only after it was blessed with the act of divine providence. In order to receive a blessing, the farmers must work hard on the field to earn the trust of the deity. Through carrying out their tasks with utmost care, a unique and distinctive view on work emerged. Although the deity of rice fields was an absolute being, for the farmers it was also a partner. It was not strange at all that the deity had been personified. In some regions, on the last day of the harvest a head of a household dressed in formal attire went to the field to meet the deity and took it to the family's home. As the entire family members awaited to welcome them, the head of the household loudly announced, "The deity has returned." The family offered the deity a hot bath and a meal prepared with the crops they have harvested. There were times when this ritual of farmers expressing their gratitude, thanking the deity for all of its hard work throughout the year, took place every year.

In those days, people saw all deities as their partners and regarded their own work as a highly spiritual act because of these relationships. Moreover, they devoted their lives continuing to work along with deities. These were truly astonishing work ethics.

Inari was the deity of rice fields, but later it also became a deity of commerce. That meant in addition to rice fields, storefronts, too, became places where people could work together with a deity. Subsequently, it expanded into retail stores and to administrative offices further spreading these work ethics. In the past, this unparalleled and perhaps even noble and sublime approach toward work was adapted and held as their tradition by people in Japan. It is not an overstatement to say the loss of such practices following the end of the war was truly devastating. I believe it is time for us to bring back and revive the traditional work ethics once again.

## 1-5 THE SOCIALITY OF BUSINESS

*C*orporate scandals are as rampant as ever. They seem unstoppable. Hardly anything shocks us anymore. The state of affairs is truly shameful. What is really happening? Through closely analyzing some of the largest corporate scandals, what I immediately thought was there is something seriously wrong with the "standards of judgment" those disgraced enterprises have.

Lately, fraud has been the most common corrupt practice. No matter what the tools of deception are – intentional mislabeling, window dressing, falsifying data and so on – they are all deliberate acts, not resulting from errors. There would no fraud without the intent to defraud. They are almost always systematic doings. An important point is that it is never a mistake of an individual.

We, the public, usually learn about the cases of corporate scandals through the media well after the wrongdoings have been uncovered and investigated. At that point, we are simply stunned at the brazenness of those involved for thinking they could get away with their crooked misconduct. I try, to the best of my ability, to think like a fraudster. But I see no way of carrying our any fraudulent activities without getting caught. I wonder why anyone can lie so blatantly. Well, there is only one possible explanation: Because it is systemic, backed by the "everyone is doing it" mentality. People find emotional relief in knowing that their superiors, whom they look up to, consented to the misdeeds and feel validated by the company they depend on. They avoid feelings of guilt by believing what they do is for the benefit of the company. If something is "for the company" or not is their standard of judgment.

Needless to say society must come before any business. But unfortunately, the idea of doing something "for society" is rarely seen at those disgraced companies. In an effort to understand what is behind this disregard, I found two underlying factors.

First is the fact that the respecting of individuals is more emphasized than the valuing the public good, sidelining the role of society as a result, in today's early childhood education which takes place during children's most formative years. Second is the absence of a basic set of "social rules" from early childhood education. Early childhood education should focus on fostering a better member of society and building the foundation necessary to be one. What constitutes the core of this foundation is a basic set of "social rules." Therefore, early childhood education should be about instilling these rules to children; however, under the current system, one can hardly tell if the teaching of the rules are even taking place. Without an adequate understanding of such rules, children cannot be expected to make sound judgments when they are older.

It goes without saying that a life consists of a series of making decisions and taking actions. Therefore, unless one understands the standards and rules of society, one cannot move forward. Without them, it is as though one is navigating though life with one's eyes closed. It is truly disconcerting how the current education system disregards this most important aspect of early education. As a result, many grow up to be full members of society with developed bodies but no concrete grasp of social standards. Because the very first set of standards they encounter is the "logic of company," they follow a profit-first approach and rely on it as the basis for making decisions and taking actions. Since they have no reasons to doubt what they are doing and their new found rule, they will continue with no reservations.

Needless to say, what should be taught in early education are the standards based on "human nature and sociality." And they are what should be established in children as a strong backbone for the standards they are going to need as an adult. This point was emphasized especially in the early childhood education system in the Edo period. While the present system is "passive education," the one in the Edo period was "active education." This is the main difference. It is not that hard to imagine the difference in outcomes the passive and active approaches could bring about. Successful education, after all, is difficult to achieve without the learners' will and desire to learn.

The basis of active learning is to let students learn what they want as much as they want at the pace they want. All students can use the same textbooks, but the speed of progress varies from one student to another.

The motivated students advance faster than those who want to take their time learning. How fast students can cover the textbook or finish the materials is not the point. What matters is whether each student really understands the materials and what he or she has "learned" has really been absorbed. Today, it seems like there is confusion about the purpose of education. Whatever the situation may be, the important thing is for children to fully grasp and attain the concept of human nature and sociality, and make it a part of their lives.

During the Edo period, children were taught that there is only one truth, and that is all that one had to know. People who are full of knowledge but do not know the one truth, or people who have a limited knowledge but have a complete understanding of the truth – it was very clear to the people at that time which one they needed to cultivate. In fact, what the children needed to learn about the foundation of human beings was quite limited.

First, children were taught "go-jyō," or the five elements: Benevolence, righteousness, ritual, wisdom and integrity. These five elements were everything they needed to know about human nature. But before the five elements, they were taught "shi-tan," or the four moral beginnings: Commiseration, a sense of shame and revulsion, a reverential attitude toward others, and a sense of right and wrong. Because shi-tan were considered as the beginning, tan, of the four virtues – benevolence, righteousness, ritual and wisdom – children were assured of grasping these concepts.

As for sociality, children were taught "go-rin," or the five cardinal relationships: A relationship between a father and a son, a ruler and a subject, a husband and a wife, an elder and a younger brother, and best friends. This was to prepare them for the three types of relationships they would encounter in society: A relationship with their superiors and the elderly, with their juniors and subordinates, and with their colleagues. "Go-kyō," or the five teachings, was what connected the human nature taught in go-jyō and the sociality taught in go-rin. Go-kyō describes the five roles of human relationships and their main attributes: Righteousness of a father, compassion of a mother, friendship of an older sibling, respect of a younger sibling, and filial piety of a child.

These are the main points of human nature and sociality that the children learned about during the Edo period. Until they were truly familiar with the concepts, the children learned them through repetition as well as lessons that took place in a real life. The Four Books and Five Classics was used as the textbook. By the time children turned fifteen-years old, which was the coming of age at that time; they had established a firm understanding of the social rules essential to a person. It is very unfortunate that today's early childhood education system does not have such a clear guideline. This is why children grow up with only a vague understanding of the social rules. And society ends up with too many adults with poor appreciation of them. If neither schools nor homes teach them to the children, at least companies need to step up to teach the young people as a part of their training for new employees.

Another contributor to the disregard of society stems from individualism in the education system. Of course there is nothing wrong with respecting individuality. Before the war, individuals were dismissed as the totalistic climate swept through Japan. Later, in reaction to this oppression the nation began to value individualism. I understand this sentiment to a degree, but I see a big problem with the way individualism has been adapted in Japan. Since the main conception of individualism seems to be self-assertion and trying to have one's own way, it has created many egotistic individuals.

There is a huge difference between the Christian nations, which individualism was modeled after in Japan, and the soil and climate of Japan in the first place. People in Christian nations live under a set of rules and principles that bind them to a life guided by a contractual relationship with their God, Jesus Christ. Therefore, the contract with God has the utmost importance in their lives. That means, under this absolute relation to God, people are required to have strong self-control and to constantly align their words and actions with this contract. We must not overlook this difference, because this is what individualism needs to stand on.

It is very rare to meet people who live by this level of self-restraint in Japan. Therefore, under the circumstances in which the education system and the social climate praise even more self-assertion and award having one's way, without exercising any meaningful restraint, there is no surprise that there are now many egotistic individuals. One may ask these people, who grew up in the environment where egotism is accepted, to put society and the public good ahead of their own needs, but they seem incapable of responding with actions.

Historically, individualism has only been seen in a very few parts of the world. People in Asia, especially in Japan, had long followed the tradition of a "family-oriented society" instead. Unless it returns to this, Japanese society will continue to face disruptions. The family had been considered as a training ground for society. One's relationships with one's father and mother, older siblings and younger siblings can help establishing relationships with one's superiors, subordinates and colleagues. The basis of sociality lies in the family.

Let us look at what society is. According to Eastern thought, society consists of two things: "Self and others." If one puts oneself ahead of everyone else, one becomes isolated. If one puts others ahead of oneself, because others mean every person besides the self, one's deeds spread endlessly. In the East, peoples' lives revolved around this idea of infiniteness. To live in this world, and to live better, one needs to establish a better relationship with others. The secret of a successful relationship is to become a "person others want to be with," not a "person others don't want to be around." What types of individuals do people wish to stay away from? A survey taken in my company shows that the respondents wish to disassociate themselves from people who are: Self-centered, self-interested, who do not share profits and or who are egocentric. Generally people want to stay away from egotistic individuals. That means becoming the opposite of an egotist is the key for leading a successful life.

Classical Chinese philosophy sought this ideal in 'the way,' or Tao – the origin of the universe. While Tao devotes all of its energy to sustain the world, to maintain order, to give birth to all things, to nurture them and to offer an abundance of fruits of its labor, it asks nothing in return nor does it demand money or favor. It dutifully performs and fulfills its given tasks and roles. Having recognized this nature of Tao as what people should learn from, the concept of "toku," or virtue, was created. The basic principle of virtue – "to give our absolute best for the benefit of others" – reflects the origin.

For a long time, the Chinese character for toku was pronounced "ikioi," which means force. What did force have to do with toku, or virtue? To be one with the state of Tao means to have no expectations, intentions, contrivance nor tactics. One's mind is free of disruptive thoughts. It is in this state of mind where one can absorb the greatest amount of the energy from heaven and earth. Also, it is in this state of mind where one's vitality reaches its peak and one can exert the most of one's energy.

When someone gives his or her absolute best to others, what would people on the receiving end feel? Naturally, there will be feelings of gratitude. If they receive more, the feelings of gratitude will become deep delight and even heighten to profoundly deep emotion. In other words, to live in harmony with Tao is to expand the 'relationships of gratitude to delight and to deep emotion.' When many people share such relationships, it is difficult to imagine that anyone would look away from those in need. In most cases, they would rush to offer hands of assistance. Many people come forward to help someone – there is no better way to express their feelings than through "action." It is a perfect way to illustrate the way we should view society.

Corporate scandals occur because companies base their judgment on making a profit, and they do anything, even lie, to avoid losing their profit. They may lie, but as the saying goes – "the net of heaven may be big, but it lets nothing through" – all of their misdeeds will be revealed in the end. Besides, given the current climate of which whistleblowing has become a widening practice and many people have become actively vigilant, anyone should really think twice about lying.

Moreover, most of the relationships businesses have exist outside the company. In other words, they deal with society the most; therefore, businesses need to remind themselves that making an enemy of society and conflicting with it could endanger their existence. Speaking from this point of view, it is crucial for businesses to manage their business from a perspective that is socially fair. I went on a little too long about corporate scandals, but I wanted to mention the basis of eliminating the scandals because no matter how many positive things I say, as long as a certain corporate culture persists, the situation will not improve.

What does it involve for businesses to actively utilize sociality? What I advocate is the "ripple-style management." The very meaning of any businesses' existence is to "offer attractive ideas to improve and change society and people's lives for the better." Businesses need to introduce innovative and ideal products and systems to the stale, old-fashioned market and society – as if to throw a stone into a calm, peaceful body of water. The stone causes ripples. In this case, ripples represent customers' sympathetic resonance. They are the words of cheers: "We have been waiting for a product like yours" and "outstanding job!" But the ripples do not simply expand, they automatically spread outward. This is exactly how one customer's sympathetic resonance reverberates to the people around it. It is an ever-growing motion where the current customers bring in new customers.

In this case, customers are acting as the company's very own salespeople. Since word-of-mouth is more effective and mightier than any media promotions, good words can spread to reach wider audiences. What this means is that this eliminates the need for businesses to have a traditional advertisement campaign. Word-of-mouth, the ripples, can travel beyond borders, spread to other countries and eventually come right back to where it started. These rebounding waves are the waves of information which contain a wealth of data – the needs and desires of the customers. Get this information and throw another stone into the water: This repetition is the business of companies.

The shared feelings and resonances are not directed only to products and services, but also to the companies themselves. These feelings could even convert their customers to the companies' workforces. These people with limited time could support the companies by becoming their shareholders, and also by actively sharing their ideas and suggestions for product developments and service improvements. As such ripples spread around the world, the businesses can have a global network of customers/shareholders, shareholders/work force, customers/workers in research and development, and users/sources of ideas. If they could manage to host a meeting once a year where all of these people came together, they would have access to years-worth of supplies of valuable ideas for their R&D, production, sales, distribution and services.

Although the companies may have a limited number of employees, because they have an astounding number of human resources that offers various expertise at all times, they can avoid problems of stagnation and decline. Engaging in business activities that are open, fair and global – this is the prime example of sociality.

## Chapter 2

## Exploring Management Approaches of the East

### 2-1 THE MEANING OF "AKEMASHITE"

"Shinnen akemashite-omedeto-gozaimasu." ("Congratulations—a new year has begun!") At the start of a new year, Japanese people exchange greetings with one another. To me, the word "akemashite" (begins) from "akeru" (to begin) seems to hold a hint for how today's society and organizations ought to be.

In Japanese the end of the month is called "misoka." It means obscurity. It describes the darkness of the night with no moon in the sky, and deriving from this, it also describes when people lack certainty or familiarity. At the end of each month, businesses balance out their books. Misoka is the day when they go through the month-end closing process by listing all the transactions that took place in the month – expenses and sales, lending and borrowing – and close the books. Similarly, people look back and recount what they did during the month, casting light onto what was obscure to them or where they lacked understanding or familiarity.

During the Edo period, a common conception was the "unity of knowledge and action." Acquiring knowledge was considered only half as good. To get full marks people had to put the knowledge into action. Therefore, as people recognized what had been obscure to them, they immediately acted on it to familiarize themselves. Because they acted on what was unknown to them as soon as they were identified, there were less obscurity and more familiarity. Essentially, this used to be the way of life where people recounted their shortcomings and identified goals for self-improvement at the end of each month before welcoming in a new month.

On ōmisoka, the last day of the year, the whole year is summed up. Listening to the bell of a Buddhist temple rung one hundred eight times, people recall the entire year reflecting on themselves. And they think about what they want to improve in the coming year – be it "I was not good at numbers," "Personal relationship with others did not go as smoothly as I'd hoped" and so on. Then, as the sun rises on the first day of the New Year, they greet each other: "Akemashite-omedeto-gozaimasu." This approach of turning "obscurity into familiarity," I believe, should be the foundation of organizational models of the future.

If we lead such a way of life, eventually the familiar surpasses the obscure. One can even expand one's knowledge to become well versed in foreign affairs or have good insight on the psychology of human behavior. Besides having academic knowledge, the expression "familiarity" seems to also connote a sort of personal capability – the likes of a broad perspective acquired through personal experience or an ability to handle any situations in an orderly fashion. We may say it represents the value of the human growth ring. Nonetheless, we can sense the underlying belief that recognizes the weight of the life of every human being in such an expression.

Management by objectives is one of the management approaches used by businesses today. While its results are mostly positive, there is a shortcoming: Its tendency to focus more on satisfying numerical targets. Numerical figures are outcomes. What generates the outcomes is personal capability. Figures cannot improve without first improving personal capacity. Therefore, I believe forward-thinking businesses need to change their approach to an "obscurity into familiarity" management approach.

For us humans, nothing is more satisfying in life than working to improve the self and enjoying the outcomes of personal growth. An approach to life that focuses on turning "obscurity into familiarity" reflects these senses of values. A lifestyle that centers on developing more familiarity is healthful, too. As familiarity also refers to bright and cheerful nature of people, there will be more optimistic seniors if people pursue this lifestyle. And because being bright and cheerful also contributes to better health, people will have more vitality as they age. Overall, there will be a surge in healthy seniors as a consequence. This explains why during the Edo period retirees and old landlords in the neighborhood were able to stay as energetic and full of vitality as the young and continue to mentor many, as a person of wisdom. It is no wonder how much they were respected and admired by society. It must have been a truly wholesome society.

Furthermore, by applying the same concept to organizations like corporations, we can discover something even more profound. Today, companies are practically disposing their most seasoned workforce, whom they have invested great time and resources, under the current mandatory retirement system. Companies are forced to let them go in their prime without utilizing these valuable resources.

To people who lead their lives turning "obscurity into familiarity," self-discipline has become a natural part of living. Their lifestyle is, in a way, very similar to the practices in the field of traditional crafts and performing arts where people work well in their seventies or even eighties to achieve the highest quality worthy of the ultimate recognition of the designation as intangible cultural heritage or a status of a living national treasure.

For companies, the existence of a large number of such seasoned and skilled workforces can enable them to take on more challenging projects easily by tapping into this wealth of knowledge and experience. They could also serve as valuable mentors or advisors to the workers, providing a solid support system to the organizations. This re-enforces companies' cooperation system that capitalizes the strength from each generation – matured, prime and rising – while revealing an ideal organizational model for an aging society.

Whether it is in society or businesses, having as many healthy and lively, knowledgeable and well-versed seniors is truly ideal for society with an aging population. Reportedly, many people are anxious about their future. I hope we can grasp the true sense of "akemashite" and incorporate its principle into our lifestyle. We can do so by illuminating what we want to improve at the end of each month for the first eleven months of the year, then by reflecting on our progress and achievements at the end of the year. And, as a new year begins, let's greet each other with the true sense of: "Shinnen akemashite-omedeto-gozaimasu."

## 2-2 KURŌTO CULTIVATION PROGRAM

There is an analytical tendency at the base of our thinking process. Analysis is a method used to seek a cause for something by taking all of its parts and elements apart in order to thoroughly examine it. Let's say a cherry tree suddenly stops bearing flowers, and we want to revive it. We start by looking into the cause. A method that first comes to mind is the analytical processes. Using this method, we examine the tree starting from its trunk then moving up to the top, studying the leaves and tips of branches along the way.

This is indeed a very effective approach. We cannot overlook the fact that we have benefitted from this method tremendously from overcoming intractable diseases to solving complex challenges. But we cannot be entirely sure whether this is truly effective for finding the cause of the sickened tree. It is because for a tree, its leaves, flowers and treetop are the least vital parts. The flowers only bloom briefly and the leaves turn colors and fall as they wither. Ever-blooming flowers and evergreens are the rather unconventional kinds. It seems quite unreasonable to try to understand the whole by looking at the weakest parts, let along to uncover the true nature. In order to really understand the true nature of things, we have to directly examine their vitality and overall conditions.

Where, then, do we need to check for the tree's vital signs? It is the roots and trunk – the organ and the main structural member. But there is a knotty problem. We cannot examine the roots from above ground. We would have to dig up the soil to expose them. It is a laborious and very inefficient undertaking. Do we have a better way to examine them? Conventionally, such burdensome processes were simply avoided or entirely omitted. We would never know how much of real nature has been left unturned as the results.

Fortunately, there is a relatively effortless way to examine the hidden roots: Bring in a person who has the ability to tell the condition of the roots without removing the earth. Believe it or not, such experts, the master caretakers of cherry trees, do exist. Supposedly, they have the ability to spot the exact location of infection with a glance. Removals of the soil from where the export indicated always reveal the infected roots. Some may wonder that these experts must be very rarer. And that is exactly the case. They are extremely rare nowadays. I believe this is where one of the problems of today's education system lurks.

It is said that every one of us is actually born with similar extraordinary abilities and wisdom. But unfortunately, it is also pointed out that most of us seldom use them in our lifetime. Especially today, a lot of efforts are being directed toward developing sophisticated analytical instruments so that we do not have to rely on our natural abilities. Although such developments may be necessary, it makes no sense if they prevent us from using our ingrained skills. We have to work on utilizing these innate abilities.

In Japan, people have long referred to experts as "kurōtos." A kurōto literally means a person who can see in the dark. Darkness or obscurity refers to things we cannot see directly such as the future and the states of places faraway. Kurōtos are people who can see and accurately foresee these things. In terms of business, kurōtos are those who are adept at foreseeing demands and achieving customer satisfaction.

The major league baseball player Ichiro Suzuki changes his position in the outfield depending on the batter. He can foresee the direction of the hit. Masters of kendo, a Japanese martial art of sword-fighting, often say they can see behind as much as the front. How can kurōtos see what is unseen? It is because they try to look at the roots. If we continue to try to look at the roots without taking our eyes off them, naturally we will become able to see them. Through persistently looking at the true nature, characteristics and personalities, we will be able to see the strengths and weaknesses, the habits and tendencies. In order to reach this point, we must look at the roots for a very long time. In other words, it becomes very important to continue to do the same things over and over, day after day.

As we look closely at the roots, the "long-term perspective" develops naturally. If we continue to look at the roots even further, we will be able to see the "diversity" and all directions. The classic Chinese texts stress these "fundamental, long-term and diverse" perspectives. These are also referred as practice, training and discipline. And they offer a new direction for corporate education. The purpose of corporate education is the cultivation of professionals. Professionals are kurōtos who are cultivated through discipline.

## 2-3 OVERCOMING DUALISM

What is the greatest challenge facing a business organization today? Perhaps, it is the search for unparalleled originality befitting the new era. Truly astonishing technological advances have made many things that were once considered impossible possible. Consequently, businesses are asked by society for more innovative, groundbreaking products and services, as well as an eye-opening, novel business model and organizational structure. In other words, businesses can no longer satisfy consumers unless they offer an element of completely unique surprise and excitement.

What is it, then, fundamentally, that businesses need to consider? To come right to the point, they need to change their way of thinking. All products and services originate in their creators' thoughts and ideas. Neither new ideas nor specifications come out of the blue. They are derived and created from the thoughts and ideas of an individual. Therefore, in order to come up with something completely new and exciting, one has to have a completely new set of thoughts and ideas. Our thinking, which has been based on Western rationalism, is being questioned today.

Dualism is a classic example of this. In dualism, a matter is divided into two sides before being discerned. It attempts to simplify a complex issue by contrasting two sides such as mind and matter, subject and object, good and evil, and dominant and subordinate. But there is a question as to whether such a simple division of a complex matter is warranted, or rather, whether it is even possible in the first place. Another problem with dualism is that it tends to exclude things that cannot be clearly divided and that cannot be expressed numerically or assessed objectively. In fact, at the moment a division is made, the two sides are immediately turned against one another. A discord created by separating the good from the bad will end up on a path where the good pushes out and takes over the bad.

Aggressive divisions like this are prevalent in business activities. For example, the division between a seller and a buyer is an adverse effect that is still alive and well. As soon as the division is made, a huge wall of awareness that prevents either side from reaching the other appears and creates a conflict between the seller and the buyer. Under such circumstances, we cannot expect a seller to engage in a business from the buyer's standpoint or offer a heartfelt service. Because all sellers are essentially buyers outside their workplace, the basic business principle to adhere to should be about creating and offering to the public what they really want. But as long as this Western dualistic approach persists, it probably will remain as an idealistic concept.

A kind of dualism also can be found in management, for instance, in the division between those that manage and those that are managed. Because this division enforces the notion where a manager is always right and the managed should always follow, the two sides do not fully interact or become united with one another.

What is disheartening about dualism is that once divided into good and bad, mind and body, leader and follower, superior or subordinate – people tend to take a side. What makes many things in this world so precious is that they are the results of various elements being intricately intertwined with one another. We disregard their inherent greatness by dividing them into two elements. Favoring only one side seems like we are distancing ourselves further away from the heart of things.

Such a way of thinking, on the contrary, is absent from Eastern philosophy and classical Chinese texts. The basis of I Ching is heni, or change, and fueki, or immutability. It is based on the idea that the world consists of two kinds of things: Things that change and things that do not. And according to its teaching there is no separation between them.

A good example is a day. As the sun rises, morning begins. As the sun continues to move across the sky, the day shifts from noon to afternoon to evening to night. There is not even a minute that escapes this change. A day, therefore, is variable. Looking at it in terms of a period of one week, on the other hand, a shift in a day – from morning to afternoon to evening to night – is repeated day in day out. Seemingly, there is no change in what happens in a day. In this case, a day is considered invariable. Neither is wrong. A day is both mutable and immutable. As this illustrates, two contradicting qualities exist through their mutually complementary relationship. Everything in this world is the result of two completely opposite and contradictory elements complementing and being united with each other. A union of conflicting and opposing elements is what completes this world.

There are examples of this in action. Asahi's Super Dry, the top selling beer in Japan, has another name: "Koku-kire beer." Koku describes the beer's richness, while kire describes sharpness in the throat. This combination is the outcome of accepting two conflicting qualities – a sharp sensation going down the throat and a deep, robust taste – rather than separating and taking a side. A pharmaceutical manufacturer implemented a system where each worker of a certain position takes turns being the leader of the group for a period of time. It is designed to ward off the adverse effects that stem from being divided into positions of a manager and the managed. The results of the workers experiencing both roles are deepened mutual understanding and an adaptation of a better management approach.

I hope businesses will offer more unique and one-of-a-kind products and services by accepting both yin and yang – the two opposing and contradictory qualities – rather than by separating them and favoring one side only.

## 2-4 "GOODNESS IS LIKE WATER" IN ACTION

"Goodness is like water." This is not an advertising slogan for sake. It is a quote from Lao-tzu. It means the most ideal way of being is to be like water.

China was the land known by the saying: "Travel by boat in the south and by horse in the north." Lives in northern China were very much nomadic, and it was where the worship of the North Star and Confucianism took hold. Southern China, with plenty of lakes, marshes and rivers, on the other hand, was more suited for the lives of agricultural people. It was where the worship of the sun and Taoism were born. That is why Taoism and water are closely associated with each other and water in many ways became a Taoist ideal.

Lao-tzu also said: "Water benefits all things and does not compete with others." Water is most essential to humans. Even though it benefits us tremendously, water does not boast about what it has done for us nor does it patronize us for it. It simply seeks lower ground and stays there, where it is often damp and undesirable. That is probably why its presence appeals to us.

Furthermore, lately water has earned a renewed respect as a healthy beverage and has become a highly competitive product. Water becomes enriched as it absorbs nutrients from various minerals and plant in its path. We could gain a lot from learning this nature of water –regard individuals and things that come into our path as our teachers and absorb new things from them. This, too, is facilitated by water's noncompetitive nature.

Over three-thousand years, this non-competitive spirit has been cherished as a basis for maintaining coexistence and harmonious relationships with others. Even in today's business environment, culture has shifted from being strictly competitive to being more alliance and collaboration oriented. This transition clearly indicates that businesses are confronted with the need for spiritual maturity.

Companies can no longer retain their absolute predominance in the marketplace or enforce their originality through their own technical capabilities nor competence alone. Companies need to form an alliance based on their specializations. This is where coexisting and maintaining harmonious relationships with other organizations becomes a key as this shift is likely to intensify. On occasion, companies will be asked to join hands with their archrivals in creating innovative products and do business together in the vast global markets.

Even within an organization, its departments need to move beyond competing with one another and focus on optimizing the company as a whole. The practice of forcing workers to compete against each other to improve their work performance has reached its limit. Distracted too much by internal contention, many companies fail to notice drastic social change and neglect to transform themselves at the social level. As a result of harsh inter-organizational contests, the number of people who have suffered from mental disorders such as nervous breakdowns, or worse, who have driven themselves to suicide have increased. These very serious problems have added sharp criticisms to this extremely high cost of doing business.

The time has come for us to face a different competitor: Ourselves and our own abilities from the day before. At times like this the "non-competitive spirit" water possesses should be adopted as a fundamental spirit of management. This spirit also shows how impossible could be possible.

Lao-tzu said: "The insubstantial can penetrate where there is no opening."

Because water has no shape of its own, it can freely travel through seemingly impossible places. There is no space water cannot find its way. No matter what shapes they are, water can fill any vessels and glasses because it has no shape of its own.

What does it mean to have no shape of our own? First, it means not putting ourselves before others. If we adamantly force our own opinions onto others, we will not be able to hear their true thoughts. We discourage them from sharing their real feelings. Therefore, it we desire to understand others, we have to put them first and really listen to what they have to say. Stubbornly clinging to our own opinions and refusing to incorporate others' views will further deepen the discord.

Sales is about listening to customers' needs and satisfying each one of them. But the sheer number of salespeople seems to misunderstand sales for asserting what the company has to say and aggressively persuading others. That is why customers cannot penetrate to the company. They are not even allowed entry.

Does this mean water teaches us to have no opinions of our own and quietly obey others? It is quite the contrary, because when situations demand water firmly asserts itself more than anything else by taking the form of a flash flood or a deluge. It has very strong opinions of its own, but it puts others first.

Furthermore, it is said that the main point of research and development is to have better understanding of the characteristics and property of materials. In order to do so, we have to listen carefully to what they want to tell us and listen to them very closely. Our needs come later. This is also the spirit of water.

Lao-tzu also said: "The softest in the world overcomes the strongest." The softest water in the world can move the hardest rock in the world at its will. Even with a very little amount, water has enough strength to make a hole in a rock by continuously dripping on the same spot over time. After three-thousand years, the time has come yet again for us to learn from water.

## 2-5  LEARNING PRODUCT PLANNING FROM ZEAMI

The classics are great for enriching our minds, but they are also valuable for practical information. They can provide their readers with essential knowledge to navigate their way through the world. When it comes to the subject of business management, the latest Western publications can undoubtedly offer great insights. However, equally valuable is to savor the Japanese classics and grasp the essentials of business management as classics are a wealth of truth.

Fūshi-kaden, a treatise written by Zeami, a great playwright and theorist of classical Japanese musical drama Noh, or Nogaku, is one such classic that offers excellent insights when read as a business management reference. Zeami uses flowers as a metaphor to explain the secrets to success in Noh in this treatise. But depending on the reader's interpretation, it reads as though he is explaining the secrets of business management.

Zeami writes: "Naturally, flowers of various trees and plants bloom respectively in their suitable time and season. That is why when they finally bloom, after having waited for the right moment, we find them unique."

By their nature, flowers bloom in accordance with the seasonal changes as if to symbolize the passage of time. People adore them because of this uniqueness that momentarily captures viewers' hearts. Zeami's observation has a compelling point; if flowers bloom all year round, they would be rather banal and uninteresting. We find them alluring because they bloom seasonally in a timely fashion and last only for a limited duration.

Zeami continues: "The same could be said for sarugaku (Noh). When the audiences find Noh unique, they find it to be interesting. The flowers, interestingness and uniqueness – these three are all the same idea."

If we replace sarugaku with a new product, new service or new business, Zeami's words means that because of its uniqueness and interestingness like blooming flowers at their peak, a new product, new service or new business gathers attention, entertains and becomes adored by many. Perhaps these words capture the importance of captivating and enthralling people's hearts, as well as summarizing the essence of business: "Delivering values." Furthermore, blooming on the premise of their eventual fall makes flowers desirable, and so does new products. New products are introduced on the premise of the emergence of even more advanced technology and sophisticated value in the future.

The idea of flowers that Zeami portrays embodies another important quality

– so-called "presence or absence of resplendence." We see it used in the expression "an actor or actress with a resplendent quality," with a meaning synonymous to having the air of brilliance or glamour, but what exactly attributes to this distinctive quality?

First is beauty. What is it, then, to be beautiful? To be beautiful is to exude elegance. What is it to exude elegance? It is to be eye-catching, captivating. In other words, there has to be remarkable "ability" to capture many people's eyes and imagination. Likewise, businesses have to possess "unique technology and ability" to maintain their operation. But possessing those alone does not necessary mean "resplendence is present." What is missing? After all, there has to be an exuberant energy to fully bloom in one's prime. To exist is to be persuasive. What is persuasive in this sense? It is about having an assertive and absolute competence and energy – a force, rather – that can hold anything down.

The same applies to businesses. Businesses that have achieved great performance and unceasingly produce one successful product after another exude definite force. According to Zeami, such "force that spurts corporate-wide" is essential to any enterprise. In other words, his words imply the real importance of "adapting to the times." Read the times carefully, alter their own technologies and know-hows to suit the needs of the times transforming them into revolutionary products, make them a great success and ride the momentum – these are what businesses need to do.

But at the same time, Zeami warns that this is also when business management needs to exercise utmost caution. He says: "Nevertheless, this flower is not a perfect flower. It is simply the flower of the moment." The outcome and achievement of this brief period does not necessarily reflect a company's true capability. One success could easily be an ephemeral hit – a "flower of the moment." This is a big hurdle and a crossroad for businesses: Depending on whether they could overcome this or not, businesses could either fizzle as an excellent-but-short lived enterprise or shine and become a truly capable one.

"The mind that believes the fleeting flower to be the perfect flower is a mind that further distances itself from the true flower." The mind which believes a momentary success of the times as a measure of one's own ability is the first step that distances any businesses from the path of becoming a truly capable enterprise. Zeami is cautioning us not to misinterpret a fluke as capability.

"Intrigued by this fleeting flower of the moment, one is unaware that the flower will soon wither." If companies remain enraptured by a fortuitous hit, their flower may never bloom. This may even lead to a loss of the flower entirely. What Zeami tries to tell us is that we should never lose sight of our ability nor forget the calm perspective that objectively checks our ability at all times. This is what the "true flower" is; to stay on a growth path that meets companies' unique ability. What, then, must we do in order to stay on the path? Zeami remarks: "This is the exact moment one must return to one's original mindset." He says the original mindset of businesses, their origin, is what could save the organization. What is the original mindset? It is the founding spirit of the company and the hardship it endured at its very beginning.

## 2-6 SUN TZU: THE ORIGIN OF STRATEGY

*M*any say that we are in the era of strategy. We are in a period of transition where no strategic thinking means no improvement in business performance. When it comes to a strategy, nothing surpasses the ancient Chinese military treatise The Art of War attributed to Sun-Tzu.
Let us explore The Art of War and seek the key to an effective strategy.

Sun Tzu begins with the following: "Warfare is a great matter to a nation. It is the matter of life and death, and the path toward safety or ruin. Hence, every detail must be carefully examined." It must be fully understood that engaging in a war is the most critical situation for any nations. It is a matter of life-or-death for the people and survival-or-destruction for the nation. Extremely cautious considerations and assessments must be given. The very first thing Sun Tzu says is that going into a war should never be taken lightly. If it can be avoided, then it should be avoided.

Manu people seem to misunderstand The Art of War as a bellicose treatise, but that is far from the case. It outlines how to avoid conflict. It teaches "how to win without engaging in a battle." Sun Tzu says: "To conquer the enemy without a battle is the best way." To conquer the enemy without a fight is the ultimate and ideal way to win. "To win one hundred victories in one hundred battles is not the best way." To engage in one hundred wars and defeat the enemy all one hundred times might seem like worthy of admiration, but it is not the best way to achieve a victory. Sun Tzu tells us not to engage in a fight, but why?

First of all, in any battle a human toll ensues on both sides. Even if one's army wins, the victory leaves animosity to the enemy and profound grief to the victor. Battles damage arms and weapons and inflict catastrophic destruction on the territory and cities of the enemy as well as the ally. Victory is often followed by the occupation of the enemy territory, but not only does rebuilding ruined cities create an enormous financial burden, this tremendous task is carried out in a land where an intense enmity is looming over. Success comes with an enormous price. To fight and conquer one hundred times over is not the best way – these words of Sun Tzu are indeed very telling.

In terms of corporate activities, this means that it is pointless for businesses to keep scrambling for market shares as a competitive strategy and fret every time they win or lose. Sun Tzu says that true success lies in either continuously holding a commanding advantage over competitors or establishing products with "Only One Quality" that nobody else in the world can match. What, then, are the important points in achieving such goals?

Sun Tzu says it is, first and foremost, to form the most powerful enterprise. What makes an enterprise the most powerful? According to Sun Tzu, its foundation is "go-ji," or the five fundamental factors: The Way, Heaven, Terrain, Leadership and Law.

The first factor is the Way. "The Way refers to uniting the hearts of the people with the hearts of their leaders." The top executives and the workers need to join their efforts to pursue shared goals. When their hearts align, "people will cast aside their fear and share their fate – to survive or to perish – with the ruler." If employees at all levels become truly united so as to share their fate, companies can become a closely-knit organization where no impending dangers will inflict even a slight fear.

The second factor is Heaven. "Heaven is night and day, cold and heat, the times and seasons." It is the opportunities endowed by Heaven. It is about constantly bringing luck to one's own army and following the flow of the times.

The third factor is Terrain. It refers to "geographical conditions – far and near, steep and plane, wide and narrow – that could separate between life and death." It means to strategize marketing that enables businesses to operate at their advantage at all times.

The fourth factor is Leadership. "Leadership refers to having qualities of wisdom, trustworthiness, benevolence, courage and strictness." After all, a leader of business must be distinguished. The qualities asked of a leader are: To be wise, to be trustworthy, to show impartial care, to be deeply courageous and to be equally strict with self and others.

The last factor is Law. "Law refers to the organization of a military, the chain of command and control of military expenditure." It refers to the importance of order and rules, and that they must be adequately followed.

In summary, in order to form the most powerful enterprise, businesses need shared goals that can unite all members of the organization. They also need to work continuously to establish favorable markets through seizing the opportunities given by Heaven, geographical advantages and momentum. Further, a competent leader, the head of the company, has to be able to fully exert his or her abilities. The most powerful is the organization that unifies these factors with clear rules, and creating such an organization is the key to "win without engaging in a battle." In other words, it is important for businesses to be seen by competitors as formidable and unbeatable enemies that discourages them from challenging their position.

If going into a war cannot be avoided no matter what, an important point to remember from Sun Tzu is this: "Soldiers are aware of hasty and precipitous warfare." Although the common interpretation is 'regardless of the level of preparedness, it is necessary to engage in a battle with haste,' this is not accurate. What Sun Tzu means is that once in a war, do not worry about clumsiness of tactics but try to end it as quickly as possible no matter what. He emphasizes the consequence of the beginning of a war.

Sun Tzu continues: "But soldiers have yet to see a successful but protracted warfare." Sun Tzu says that he had never seen a protracted war that was gainful. What does this mean for businesses? "One who knows the enemy and knows oneself needs not fear the finding of oneself in the danger of one hundred battles." According to Sun Tzu, the key to a successful business is to fully understand who the customers are and their needs and wishes, as well as how businesses themselves respond and cater to them.

## 2-7 LEADING A FULFILLED LIFE

The foundation of human beings is how we conduct ourselves as humans and how we lead our lives. Yet, this most basic essence of life has been neglected lately as many have become too quick to seek instant gratification. We need to turn this around. Here, let us explore how classic Chinese texts consider the fundamentals of being human.

Classic Chinese texts begin with the teaching of "filial piety." Who do we meet first when we come into this world? Our mother and father. There is no meeting more important than this one. It bears a deep and significant meaning. First, we learn about woman from our mother. And we receive unconditional love and affection from her. Likewise, we learn about man from our father and receive love that arises from righteousness and morality. The world is composed of women and men; therefore, having an adequate understanding of the attributes of both sexes becomes immensely valuable in our lives later on.

In addition, we learn what "selflessness" is from our parents. We become familiar with love and deeds that seek nothing in return and the manners and behaviors in which our parents carry themselves when offering them to others. The more we grasp what selfless love and deeds are, the more we become aware of what self-centeredness is. Eventually, we become able to recognize the true intent and value of love and deeds others impart to us. This is because observing the altruistic acts of our mother and father over time forms the basis and standard of identifying them. In other words we become undeceivable, which is the most important quality in life. That is why our very first encounter is with our parents and we live together for many years. These bases of human beings are collectively called "filial piety."

Filial duty refers to children's devotion and respect toward their parents. It is a manifestation of the great debt of gratitude we have toward our parents for having shaped our bases as human beings. The love and respect we harbor through the relationship with our parents will flourish when we engage with our superiors in the workplace. Even our relationships with our siblings are considered as opportunities to prepare our minds for the future encounters with our colleagues and subordinates.

Once the base has been set, what comes next? Shōgaku, a textbook used in childhood education until the Edo period, contains the following passage: "The order of heaven is called nature. To follow nature is called the way. To pursue the way is called learning." Education is all about self-discovery of the origin of human beings – innate human nature and qualities that we cannot be without – developing a sense of exaltation, and understanding and pursuing the order of this world.

What, then, are the origin and nature of human beings? These are: To sympathize with others in need (sokuin or compassion), to be ashamed of one's vices and detesting other's misdeeds (shūo or the sense of shame), to give humbly to others (jijō or a reverential attitude toward others) and to determine whether something is rational (zehi or the sense of right and wrong). Unlike knowledge which we can cram into ourselves, our nature is something we can only realize through self-reflection. As we get older, our nature is said to develop into "jin-gi-rei-chi" or benevolence, righteousness, courtesy and wisdom.

Shōgaku also emphasizes "seiso, ōtai, shintai," or cleanliness, conduct toward others and one's action, as the necessary qualities to acquire during the early childhood. Cleanliness refers to the ability to maintain an uncluttered and orderly mind. Even if we become overwhelmed by difficult and serious situations, it will serve us to composedly find a resolution. As for conducts toward others, our lives begin and end with dealing with others. Be it people, matters or situations, the ability to deal with them will enable us swiftly solve the mountain of problems at hand. Then, there is action. Including our course of action – whether to advance or to retreat – life is the accumulation of decisions we make to either continue or discontinue. In Shōgaku, firmly acquiring the essentials of these three qualities was considered as the core of childhood education.

What follows after the foundation for human beings has been firmly established? "To learn and to practice what you learned are a great pleasure." Shōgaku explains that life is about learning and a continuation of learning. But what is more important is to acquire something. To acquire is to practice what you have learned over and over until achieving mastery. Learning something is only half as good. We will be able to master it only after acquiring through actual practices. According to Shōgaku, the joy of learning and mastering, which is to say to see our improved self is the greatest joy of our lives.

How one shapes one's foundation as a human being during early childhood is considered as a great importance in life. And this is regarded as the basis for leading a good life. Today, an extended period of time – almost twenty years from kindergarten to university – is spent in forming the foundation. But its primary purpose has become vague to say the least. Early childhood education should focus on "raising a truly capable being," as it is very important for children to acquire the fundamental ability to lead an enjoyable life during this period.

As for how to lead the subsequent life there is a saying from The Analects of Confucius that has served as an example for thousands of years: "At fifteen, set your heart on learning. At thirty, stand on your own. At forty, have no doubts. At fifty, understand your fate. At sixty, willingly give an ear to others. At seventy, arrive at the state where you can follow your heart's desire without transgressing the moral standards." Despite being free and having uninhibited manners in conducting oneself, one causes no trouble to society and others because of the solid foundation one has; this is the goal in life. In a different perspective, perhaps it can also be summarized as this Taoist aphorism: "One who knows that enough is enough will always have enough." People who are truly rich in life are those who lead their lives with no discontent but with a heart of tremendous gratitude.

## 2-8 THE ESSENCE OF CORPORATE SOCIAL RESPONSIBILITY

Lately, calls for a healthy relationship between corporations and society, also known as corporate social responsibility (CSR) have grown and spread globally. But a similar idea had already been demonstrated three thousand years ago in Confucian thought. It had concisely introduced what should be the core of CRS.

For example, Mencius warns: "Your Majesty, why must you speak of profit? Only benevolence and righteousness are necessary to rule the nation." If one truly desires a company's growth and success, concerning oneself only about profit will result in the opposite, unwanted outcome. Benevolence and righteousness are what one needs to concern oneself with. That is because, Mencius continues: "If righteousness is put after profit, the enemy will remain discontent unless they seize it all." If all one thinks of is profit and one's mind is occupied by it, one can no longer be satisfied unless seizing more from others.

In other words, if one becomes too consumed by making profit, because profit by nature makes people desire more than what they already have, eventually one will try to satisfy the desire by any means – even if it means to take from others. 'Others' include not only the people outside one's company but also one's superiors, subordinates and colleagues. What this leads to are competitions among colleagues over profit and credit for job performances within the company. Clearly, no growth is in the future of such organizations. Moreover, as one becomes used to the idea of taking profit that belong to others, one will not hesitate to engage in deceptions and lies, whitewash and fraud, possibly pushing the business to its demise.

We need to better understand the meaning of the Chinese character for "profit": "利" (pronounced li). The left side of the character "禾" represents rice while the right side "刂" represents a sharp knife. In other words, "利" represents rice harvesting. Needless to say, the time for rice harvesting does not arrive magically. It begins with preparing soil for rice seedlings, and after year-long tending harvesting time finally arrives. That means the most critical stage for growing rice is the cultivation. What matters the most is how much effort is directed during this phase so the plants will bear heavy beads of rice. The harvesting is not the most important stage. Therefore, "利," or profit, is the manifestation of the labor; the results of nurturing and tending the crops throughout the entire year as if they were their own child.

In other words, whatever we are dealing with – be it personal relationships or objects – unless we put love and care into it, an outcome will be unsatisfying. Similarly, unless we provide essential nutrients and tending, an outcome will be also unsatisfying. Conversely, we need to carefully remove what hinders or damages its growth. Profit is the reward we earn in return for our time and efforts.

The love and care we offer to others are called "jin," or benevolence, and providing essential nutrients and tending is called "gi," or righteousness. Mencius says that profit will only follow our sincere offering of jin-gi. In other words, because profit is something to be earned as a result of rendering jin-gi, our utmost effort should be on offering them to others. Only after establishing a business which emphasizes jin-gi and where superior benevolence and righteousness is present, do large profits become attainable. We could also say that joy and pleasure as human beings lies in the rendering of jin-gi. Mencius points out that true pleasure is found in the acts of nurturing something or fostering businesses and enterprises themselves, and not only in the resulting profit or performances.

Needless to say, Confucianism does not deny profit. It acknowledges profit as necessity. But it stresses that the more we desire profit and wish to multiply it, the more benevolence and righteousness we need to put forth. In The Great Learning, one of the Four Books in Confucianism, there is a passage that illustrates this idea: "Virtue is the root; wealth is the branches."

The importance of this idea was also emphasized by Eiichi Shibusawa, the late Japanese industrialist who is well-known for his book Rongo to Soroban ("The Analects and the Abacus"). He says: "The Analects, namely morals and ethics and social responsibility of a corporation, and abacus, namely business and commercial activities and profitability, cannot exist one without the other. They have a mutually complementary relationship with each other." Shibusawa's idea has roots in the concept of yin and yang of classic Chinese philosophy where yin and yang are considered as complementary opposites and mutually indispensable to one another.

In the present day, businesses often apply the Western idea of "dualism" in their thinking – separating a matter into two opposing sides and choosing one side to give priority over another. But Shibusawa was different. He believed that corporate activities are about serving and offering values to society. Only after their fulfillment, businesses receive money and value as a token of sympathy and unity from society, subsequently increasing their sales and profit. Businesses and society are in a mutually supportive relationship, and the two are neither too close nor too distant from one another. Shibusawa emphasizes that an economy becomes robust as a mutually supportive relationship between businesses and society only with the presence of virtue, whereas virtue spreads only after society gains stability through economic activities.

Furthermore, Shibusawa says the key to successful business management is for businesses to cherish the minds that cares for the world and put in action to improve the lives of others through business practices. He expresses this idea as "shikon-shosai" – having a samurai's spirit and a merchant's business sense.

A spirit of samurai is necessary to be a part of human society, but that alone is not enough. Operating solely on this frame of mind could lead to a hardship on the financial front. Therefore, the business sense of a merchant must also be present. And because virtue has been at its basis, there should be no tolerance for immorality, deception, levity and frivolity. I believe we are at the juncture where we should advocate to the world the concept of corporate social responsibility through the traditional spirit of Japan – "Shikon-shosai," an Eastern kind of "dualism" based on the merging of the samurai spirit with a merchant's business sense.

## 2-9  THE TEACHINGS OF TAOISM

The biggest problem surrounding today's corporate management is that there is no management philosophy that can be used as the foundation of the reality for the rapidly changing twenty-first century business environment. We may say that reality has moved ahead before a proper set of principles has been established.

For instance, under the current corporate management system, businesses – even fledging start-ups – have already extended their operation to the global markets such as China and Singapore. For medium-sized or larger companies, having their supply and customer bases worldwide has become the norm. What this shift indicates is that there is a demand for businesses to adopt a new global perspective.

But in order to effectively employ such a perspective, businesses need to operate with an even broader perspective that allows them to observe the world objectively, like an astronaut in space looking at the earth as a globe hovering in outer space. Why? The reason becomes clear when we consider the environmental problems we are currently faced with. China's headache over its domestic emission issues, for example, could easily spread globally. Therefore, each

and every automotive manufacturer needs to pay attention and understand the patterns of atmospheric circulation. If they continue to focus on selling more cars while ignoring the risk, although their sales may spike, they will have to bear the burden of their sins as accomplices in harming the planet.
The same goes for the widely known problems of depletion in the ozone layer and global warming.

But unfortunately, we are not equipped with a present-day management philosophy that encompasses a universal perspective. Yet, the reality of business operations has already moved ahead to the next stage. The essential business assets have become controlled and managed in the form of "invisible assets" or "intangible assets." Invisible and intangible resources have become mainstream as resources such as intellectual assets provide the capital for business operations. However, current management philosophy is still limited to dealing with the visible and the tangible. It is because intangible assets had not been considered as scientific in Western thought. In addition, there is also mismanagement of the "tacit knowledge" of masterships and expertism – other major resources sustaining business activities. What is asked of a business organization today is an organic quality as if it were a "single living body." An organization is faced with the need to be a single life form that is made up of cells equipped with a brain and mind, not just an entity made up of its parts. Businesses are also expected to be a collective human force that is based on the joys of their workers' lives, offer products, values, created in such an environment and is compelled to engender the joys of life in their customers. But even here, the outdated idea characterized as the "mechanistic view of the corporation" has persisted at the base creating a large gap between what is taking place and the need of the times. To name just a few, there are various challenges facing businesses at present.

Among the many classic Chinese texts, a rather unique set of beliefs is Taoism. The core of Taoist beliefs is "nothingness." Nothingness lies on the other side of being – what we see, hear and touch. According to Taoism, in order to see the unseeable, hear the inaudible and touch the untouchable, we need to fully understand the existence of nothingness. And we need to do so not through processing knowledge in our heads, but through acquiring and realizing from actual experiences.

"All things in the world are created out of being, and being is created out of nothingness."

Depending on how we see being – as simply what it is or as the consequence of the infinite and limitless world of nothingness that exists beyond – the perception of it becomes completely different. An example to illustrate this is how one thinks of customers. Customers are not mere bodies. Although they may not tell stories, express or plead their opinions, and remain rather silent, they possess a surprising range of emotions, wishes and desires. The same can be said for workers, suppliers and stockholders. Once nothingness is truly understood, the perception of others changes. And this change leads to changes in how one treats others and the quality of services.

The idea of "all creations are equal" exists at the root of Taoism. It believes all creations in this world are one and the same. There is no distinction of ranks or a dividing line between rich and poor. Because there is no separation or discrimination among people, a circle of sympathy and unity expands more freely. The foundation of nothingness, the origin of the Universe is called "Tao." By aligning the way of self to the way of Tao, one becomes able to grasp the concept of being as well as what is beyond: Nothingness. Through this, Taoist teaching says, "repression, stagnation and hesitation" will be detached from one's actions, enabling one to achieve the state of harmony.

"With no intervention, there is nothing that cannot be accomplished." This means that there is nothing that is unattainable if things are developed through effectively utilizing careful observation of the trend of the world and the inclination of an organization, instead of forceful artificial interventions.

In contrast to Taoism, other thoughts are often based on who we are as individuals (selves) in our relationship to society. Taoist thought, in a sense, teaches us who we are as individuals in our relationship to the Universe as if grasping the whole from the outer bounds of the notion of society. It also perceives the complimentary relationship between the microcosm within us and the Universe that unceasingly sustains our lives as the source of life of all creations in this world. In other words, Taoism is the thought that encompasses a microcosmic perspective and an emphasis on life.

Furthermore, there is another distinction worth noting. Not a single proper noun appears in the text the Tao Te Ching. In the case of other teachings, such as the Sōtō school of Zen in Japanese Buddhism, in order for followers to arrive at truth, they must go through the mediators – first, Dōgen Zenji, the Zen priest and the founder of the Sōtō school, then the Buddha. Or in the case of traditional Chinese thought, Confucianism, the followers must go through Confucius or his disciples. In contrast, Lao-tzu leads us directly to face the truth, Tao, and allows us to experience it firsthand. Perhaps, the twenty-first century management philosophy should incorporate the profound yet ethereal and calm rationality Taoism embraces.

## 2-10 LEARNING CREATIVITY FROM MATSUO BASHŌ

For businesses, their products are their lives. No matter how outstanding their sales forces and management capabilities may be, without a good solid product they cannot be put to full use. How is a good solid product created? It comes from a traditional idea of creativity that businesses need to have. What does this traditional idea of creativity look like? We can turn to Matsuo Bashō, the late renowned Japanese poet, for the answer.

Bashō had created scores of haiku poems over the course of his lifetime. Most of his work are praised and regarded as masterpieces. They are still well-received and enjoyed by many today. In other words, Bashō is the originator of enduring best-selling products. How did Bashō achieve such a great feat? What attributed to his accomplishment? It was due to his unique concept of creativity. Perhaps this is what those who are working in product development could learn from the most.

The concept of creativity perceived by Bashō is well known as "fueki-ryūkō." What is fueki-ryūkō? The state of perpetual fueki, or immutability, is a fundamental principle. It is the truth beyond new and old, beauty and greatness that transcends time. Bashō's haikus embody this very idea, which is why they have not lost their contemporary freshness even to this day. His works were created upon a well-founded fueki. In terms of product development, fueki refers to the outstanding functionality of a product. In the case of a bicycle, for instance, it is the great performance such as smoothness of the ride or lightness of the pedal.

Without superb functionality, a foundation cannot be set.

Ryūkō, or prevailing trends of a given time, on the other hand, refers to the transition and changes of the times. After all, unless products conform to the trend of the moment, they cannot captivate the heart of the people.

When yin and yang, fueki and ryūkō are in harmony with one another, "fūga no makoto," or the quintessence of creativity, emerges. The concept of creativity based on the concept of yin and yang is an intellectual asset of mankind that has been continuously handed down from ancient China. Everything in this world is the result of perfectly harmonizing yin and yang. Because they appear to be contrary forces to each other, Western science sees yin and yang to be contradictory, and tends to separate such a pair to choose one over the other. But Eastern beliefs traditionally see this approach to results as incompleteness, as only the half of a whole is considered.

An example to illustrate this is a natural hot spring. Hot springs consist of two contrary elements: Fire and water. In modern thinking, a discussion of hot springs would veer toward focusing on either fire or water, diverging far from completeness as a result. On the contrary, Eastern thinking considers that taking two elements as contrary would only lead to such separation; it recognizes them as complementary opposites. Because the nature of a complementary relationship is about supply what the other is missing, naturally opposing elements have to be brought in. Once they are, the relationship becomes complete. In terms of the concept of creativity, this means to always keep conflicting and opposing qualities in mind, treat them as complementary to one another and think how they can be melded together.

Bashō says: "In the world of haiku, a poet conforms himself to the workings of nature and takes pleasure in the changes of the four seasons." Fūga no makoto, or the quintessence of creativity, is the order of this world; it was the poetic inspiration or the quintessence of poetic sentiment in Bashō's case. We could even call it a pursuit of perfection.

If we wish to create something of this nature, Bashō says, we must conform ourselves to nature. Nature is the energy of creation that lies at the root of this world. For people, it is a will and desire to create. The essence of this world is the energy and workings of "creation and evolution" which unceasingly gives birth to all creations. Because of these energy and workings, everything from humans, animals, plants to minerals ceaselessly comes into existence. Nature is the most important thing that the world cannot be sustained without.

Nature is also present in our body as it is a microcosm of the larger world. What we need is more of the spirit of the nature within us – the poetic inspiration and sentiment in the case of Bashō and the spirit of product development for those who are tasked with creating new products.

The last part of Bashō's words, "take pleasure in the changes of the four seasons," reflects that the world is always changing without ever stalling. The most significant aspect of change is that everything is always new and different. This very moment is different from the moment of a second ago. Now is a new moment and it is brand new. This is the same sentiment as seen in Hōjōki written by the Japanese poet Kamo no Chōmei: "The current of a river does not halt. And the water that is flowing at this moment is not the same water that passed here a moment ago." A river may appear the same as it was a second ago, but it is a different river – a completely new sight with completely new scenery. If we could appreciate every moment as such, we will open ourselves to new excitements that will inspire our inner poet, or developer, to create something new.

What would happen after achieving such a state of mind? Bashō says: "There is nothing you can see that is not a flower; there is nothing you can think that is not the moon." Everything we see becomes a subject of poetry – the moon, flowers, and other beauties of nature. Therefore, ideas for new creations become inexhaustible. That means as long as one holds this concept of creativity, a poet will never find oneself in a rut, or a developer will never run out of ideas for new products. Because the source of inspirations appears ceaselessly right in front of our eyes, there will always be new stimuli for creativity, and creative impasses will be unheard of.

What comes next? One becomes closer to the quintessence of "fueki-ryūkō" and becomes one with the very origin of this world, the originator of all creations.

## 2-11 LEARNING WORK ETHICS FROM SEN NO RIKYŪ

Unlike the time when traces of steep economic growth were felt, workers' professional awareness affects their quality of work in today's more stable and mature economy. In other words, the workers' frame of mind when they perform their task matters. The more offering heartfelt and cordial services becomes emphasized, the more what is on the minds of those that provide these services matters. Moreover, the more advanced one's job becomes or the more responsibility one assumes, the more one's perspective in life becomes apparent through one's professional approach. What becomes important, then, is the concept of 'the way,' or the Tao.

Under this concept, bujuitsu transforms into budō, or the martial way, sho transforms into shodō, or the way of writing and ikebana, flower arrangement, becomes kadō, or the way of flowers. A chef would follow the way of cooking, a baseball player the way of baseball and a worker the way of business. What is 'the way' anyway?

When Buddhism and Confucianism were first introduced to Japan centuries ago, they were called hotoke-no-michi (the way of the Buddha) or ten-no-michi (the way of heaven). And people referred to entering into these beliefs and practices nyūdō – entering the way. Soon this idea of entering into a way was adapted to specialized fields such as kyūshi-no-michi (the way of archery) and kanen-no-michi (the way of instruments). During the Edo period, the expression and philosophy – budō, shodō, kadō and kōdō (the way of incense) – further extended to the realms of arts and entertainment. How did it become so widely accepted in Japan? It is because the concept of the way, or the Tao, was suited perfectly for the sensibilities of the Japanese people.

What, then, is the concept of the way, or the Tao? In ancient Chinese philosophy, the Tao represents the ideal and model of the world. It also represents the process of acquiring self-discipline to reach this level, or the stages of the actual practice and cultivation. To live in accordance with the Tao is to lead a way of life in which one strives to strengthen one's ability in a specialized field. This way of life has long been relished in the spirit of the Japanese people.

Sen no Rikyū, the master of chanoyu, or the tea ceremony, described this perfectly: "The spirit of chanoyu is about achieving enlightenment through mastering the practice of tea ceremony as though you are devoting yourself to the Buddhist practices." The reason why we work is not merely for making a living. Rather, we do so for the reason of the attainment of enlightenment through engaging in our work as if it is a form of Buddhist practices. I believe the prevalence of this practice among the Japanese people has contributed to the nation's high intelligence.

Till this day, this spirit has run deep among Japanese artisans, and Japan has prided itself on the distinguished skills and techniques recognized as its forte. Even in a corporate environment, there used to be people who possessed such spirit in every division not long ago. But unfortunately, this tradition appears to be disappearing amid the rapid changes the nation has experienced in the past decade. That is why we need to revisit Rikyū's words. His work ethic is truly incredible and exemplary.

What kind of Buddhist practices did Rikyū refer to? Following the earlier remark he said, "A house is good enough as long as the roof does not leak, and a meal is good enough as long as we do not starve. These are the teachings of the Buddha as well as the intended purpose of chanoyu." Living in an extravagant mansion and consuming gourmet food are not the ultimate goals in life. We may focus on pursuing such material satisfaction, but because of its elusive nature, as soon as we attain one thing we will always be seeking for more. Instead, what we need to pursue is emotional satisfaction.

Today, shows about gourmet food dominate the TV. They try to appeal to the viewers about how amazing the constant pursuit of tasty foods is. Other oversold programs are those that showcase lavish mansions, in which the owners of the estates are often portrayed as the winners in life. These portrayals of certain work ethics and outlooks on life can have a strong affect on all the viewers, not just the children. Soon, their work ethic will resemble very little of what Rikyū taught, and Japan's diligent and earnest attitude toward labor could face the danger of collapsing before we know it. At a minimum, a social climate that values emotional satisfaction alongside the promotion of material benefits needs to be restored.

An amazing thing about the work ethic Rikyū established is that not only does it express an idealistic view but it also touches on how to deal with everyday situations. When he was asked about the secret of performing chanoyu in summer and winter, Rikyū replied: "The secret of wabi-cha is to perform the ceremony as if to bring coolness in summer and warmth in winter." Unsatisfied by the response he was asked again, "That is obvious. Isn't that what everyone does?" Rikyū's response to this was, "If you could do this so well at a ceremony you host, I would like to become your apprentice right away." Rikyū conveys the importance of paying attention to what is perceived as 'obvious.'

Although some people may think "Buddhist practices" involve doing something difficult or demanding, this is not correct. The path to reach enlightenment is about tending to the ordinary aspects of life wholeheartedly and with the best of intentions. There is an anecdote about Jukō Murata, the founder of wabi-cha and a teacher of Rikyū that illustrates this point. One day Tamura visited a Japanese Zen Buddhist monk Ikkyū, hoping that Ikkyū would take him in for Zen practice at his temple. But Ikkyū bellowed out at Tamura, "The teachings of Buddhism lies in the practice of chanoyu!" No matter what work we do, according to Ikkyū, if we set our mind to it, it could be a Buddhist practice.

## 2-12 LEARNING SALES STRATEGIES FROM MUSASHI MIYAMOTO

Go Rin No Sho (The Book of Five Rings) written by the legendary swordsman Musashi Miyamoto considers various fundamentals of swordsmanship. Intriguingly, Go Rin No Sho is not only valuable as a martial arts text, but also as a management manual. It is, in this aspect, very similar to Fushikaden written by Zeami. Musashi details in this book of tactics the secrets he mastered through years of training and his warfare experience. In this sense, it is a text on strategy. Therefore, approached as a practical guide to sales strategy, we can gain highly constructive information relevant to today's business environment.

In the introduction, Musashi writes: "Tactics are the principles of a samurai.

Commanders in particular should put the tactics into practice while soldiers should be familiar with them. In the present day, I see no samurai with a true understanding of tactics." Tactics, or strategies, is essential for samurais and, in today's case, businesspersons. This knowledge is essential for commanders and executives as well as soldiers and rank-and-file workers, yet there are hardly any businesspersons who have concretely acquired such tactics.

Musashi continues: "Because of their beliefs, it appears as though the thought of honorable demise is always with samurais. But death comes for everyone, not only for samurais. From monks, homemakers to farmers, there is no difference in facing the obligations, having a sense of honor, or wishing to decide where to draw their last breath." Often, samurais' resolves are associated with their sacrificing their lives rather readily. But the fact is it does cross the minds of many including monks, homemakers and farmers. Therefore, what makes samurais, or businesspersons, distinctive is whether they understand the tactics. In other words, having a resolve to work hard is not enough. They need strategic knowledge and practical ability because only working hard does not set them apart.

This is very important to keep in mind because although sales departments and salespersons tend to rely on drive and fortitude and emphasize mental strength, Musashi says we cannot win with this approach. He emphasizes the importance of understanding strategy. And surely Musashi does not overlook to cautioning us against all-too-common pitfalls. Quite naturally, even a slight exposure to strategic thinking could make people boast or act out on their newly acquired knowledge. Even more common is overlooking their strategic capabilities while overstating the names of universities they went to. To this, Musashi warns: "A little learning is indeed a dangerous thing. Concerning the way of tactics in particular, people are inclined to embellish it, make it grander and boast their newly acquired knowledge. They would even open a dojo or two to instill the knowledge in others and themselves, and try to prosper from it." Musashi warns that the most dangerous is focusing too much on fame over real ability and style over substance through deliberately exaggerated and ostentatious displays of one's knowledge, or excessive focus on selling the name of businesses.

When it comes to actual warfare, what does Musashi say we need to be cautious of? He begins with a basic premise: "What carpenters need to know is the importance of owning very sharp tools and honing them often in their spare moments." Using carpenters as an example, he explains that it is ingrained in expert craftspeople to take excellent care of their tools. Sharpness is so vital that without it our work suffers. That is why it is crucial for us to hone and polish our instruments even in our spare time.

Sales are perceived as a kind of all-talk, all-pitch job, but surprisingly top salespersons are often reserved and even shy. The secret of their success lies in their incredible efforts in trying to overcome their insecurity in speaking by working diligently on their tools – their sales tools. They make sure they have well-honed sales tools ready at hand and constantly re-examine, sharpen and polish the tools to make them even more effective.

The next important thing, Musashi says, is rhythm. "Although everything has its own rhythm, particularly the rhythm of tactics, mastering it depends on training." Rhythm and tempo reside in all things. They are vital especially for tactics and there is no other way to acquire them but through cultivation and practice. The Major League baseball player Ichiro Suzuki seems as though he is already in his own rhythm before he steps into the batter's box. In other words, an important thing is to be able to get into the rhythm we are most comfortable with at anytime and make others attune to it. An effect of this is quite obvious if we think of the times things did not go quite the way we had hoped. Our missteps were often the results of failing to fully get into our own rhythm.

Aside from noting the way of salespersons, Musashi offers to managers management advice on how to effectively run their sales staff. "… just as commanding people to build houses, the responsibilities of a chief of carpenters and the one of samurais are the same. When building houses, the chief pays close attention to every piece of wood to determine its best use … and when assigning tasks, the chief carefully considers each worker's skill levels … When tasks are delegated according to the right skill sets, works become accomplished smoothly." The best location and the most suitable application for wood can be determined through close examination and observation of its quality. By understanding each carpenter's skill level and assigning tasks accordingly, the work will be completed more effectively and smoothly. Essentially, according to Musashi, management is about knowing the individuals very well and appointing the right person in the right place.

## 2-13 AN INVITATION TO INFINITE THINKING

What is the greatest challenge facing today's businesspeople? How to devise a new form and a shape – for the current state of business in particular – with a completely new way of thinking and fresh ideas, is one of them. In terms of scope of activities, services provided lately by some local governments to their residents are very comprehensive. So much so that sometimes their values even exceed what commercial businesses offer. In addition, some NPOs have taken on profit-making businesses – traditionally the domain of for-profits – giving them a unique spin transpired by thinking from a different angle and out-of-the-box ideas. The cases of effective efforts such as these make many of us question the role of commercial businesses. It is the current state of businesses that is being called into question.

It has been quite some time since many said that we are at a turning point. We are finally at the moment to go around the final bend and enjoy new scenery. History is unfolding, taking us another step forward. We are entering a new era. What is very important now is our frame of mind or way of thinking, because unless we have a new way of thinking, no new forms or shapes will be created. So many different approaches have already been introduced. The so-called niche thinking, a way of maximizing our thinking by effectively utilizing every free moment to contemplate on ideas, and reversal thinking, a way of looking at problems or situations from a perspective that may defy usual thinking patterns and logic, are among them. But none seems to have taken root. Perhaps it is because these approaches are not reinforced by deep ideological thoughts and not likely to press keenly for the truth.

What we can turn to, then, is Taoism. Taoist thinking is epitomized by the saying: "All things in the world are created out of being, and being is created out of nothingness." Although all things in this world originate in being – something we can see, hear and touch – being comes from nothingness – something intangible we cannot see. The approaches like Taoism are important today because a real transformation of the world of being cannot take place in itself, where the fundamental perspective is the same. Therefore, the more we seek to change the world of being, the more we need to stand in its origin – the world of nothingness – and reassess the world of being from a different perspective.

Being is finite; therefore, the idea itself has a limit and a boundary. But once we are in the world of nothingness and think from the place where everything is infinite, we will have infinite access to completely new ideas and ways of thinking. What do we need to do to be in the world of nothingness? First, we need to understand what nothingness is.

In Taoism, the origin of the universe is called the way, or Tao. This is how the philosophy of Lao-tzu and Chuang-tzu became known as Taoism. According to Taoism, the way, or Tao, is "something undefined and complete which came into existence before heaven and earth." That means the Tao, whose existence preceded the creation of heaven and earth, is the origin of all things. The Tao is also described as "silent and formless," "profound yet subtle," and "faint and undefined." Intangible and soundless means it is not confined to a particular form or voice. It has complete freedom. Because we do not know its true identity, the more vague and indefinable it is the greater its scale and possibilities appear to us.

Tao's formless and silent nature is in common with infinitude, suggesting the possibilities of infinite thinking. Such qualities of Tao also reflects the state of our mind, suggesting living in accordance with the way of the universe, therefore, to live by the laws of nature is the way to lead a life that never comes to a standstill. Here, nature includes the universe, earth, all natural creations and also a natural mind.

A natural mind is mui, or wu wei. Only at the state of mui – a mind that is free of artificiality and deceptive intentions – can we finally be one with heaven and earth, ready to receive their energy. A saying goes: "There is nothing one cannot accomplish in the state of mui." Anything is possible once we achieve mui. In other words, living by the laws of heaven and earth is the way we should lead our life. And doing so is also how the way of heaven and the way of humans become one, achieving the mastery of Tao – the origin of all things. Once this is achieved, it is said that we can overcome even the contradictions of the world. When the contradictions of yin and yang are harmonized, they generate what the way, or Tao, is: Vigor and energy.

What those of us who are a part of a business organization need to do now is to overcome various contradictions surrounding our business activities. Otherwise, challenges we presently face – creating a successful mechanism where the more contributions companies make to the society, the more profit they make, or a structure where the more satisfied workers are, the more customer value increases – will not find any resolutions. In order to conceive new ideas, we need to find a way of thinking that transcends the present situation. That is what the thinking of nothingness is, and, by achieving this way of thinking, we will be able to acquire infinite thoughts.

A mirror is often used to describe the infinity of Tao. There is no ulterior motive, rigid insistence or ego found on the mirror itself. It is also free of obligations and artificiality. Because it is devoid of all things, no image is on its surface. That is why a mirror is capable of infinitely reflecting anything that stands in front of it. Similarly, as long as something is on our mind, our mind becomes bound and consumed by what already occupies it. But as soon as our mind becomes free from obstructive thoughts, infinite forms and shapes, and ideas and inspirations spring out in our mind. By being selfless and free of all distracting and hindering thoughts, instead of being attached too much to the past, present, our opinions, or knowledge, we will be able to draw forth unlimited inspirations.

## 2-14 HUMAN POTENTIAL IS THE KEY TO SUCCESS

Recently, the cultivation of human potential has emerged as an important objective in corporate education and training. Its popularity is not limited to just business communities, however. Japan's Ministry of Education has also stressed its importance, drawing the attention of educational institutions. Why is there so much focus on human potential today?

Presumably, many people have come to realize, after experiencing many social turbulences and a tough shifting corporate environment, that conventional ideas and techniques are not working so well. And they have become more keenly aware that when two people come face to face, what determines who has the upper hand is the level of their competence. When things happen even more globally, we have to build relationships with people of different nationalities and ethnicities. In such times what we can count on, above all else, is human potential.

What, then, is human potential? It is probably easier to revisit history than trying to understand it conceptually. In recent Japanese history, one event which is considered to have exhibited the power of human potential is the so-called "bloodless surrender of Edo castle," where negotiations between two samurais, Saigō Nanshū and Katsu Kaishū, took place in 1868.

Katsu recalled how the negotiations began. "The imperial forces poured into the city of Shinagawa surrounding Edo. Although they were ready to advance to Edo castle, after receiving my letter, Saigō made a decision to restrain his army and visit me in order to negotiate. Given the situation, it was not something one would usually do."

The two men had already known each other prior to this incident. When Katsu, the head of the shogunate army, was ordered to control the opposition forces' imminent surge, he chose to negotiate with Saigō, rather than to fight. This was the first display of human potential. Katsu's human potential led him to select Saigō to negotiate with, and Saigō's human potential led Katsu to choose Saigō to negotiate with – this was a confrontation of one man's potential against the other.

On the day of the negotiation, Katsu made his way to the meeting place. Katsu continued: "After awhile, Saigō appeared through the garden. He was dressed in old clothes and wore wooden clogs from his hometown. He had his faithful servant Kumajirō in tow. Even though he arrived late, he approached the house as if nothing was amiss. He casually said 'sorry for being late' as he entered the sitting room. His mannerism did not allude to the gravity of what was about to take place at all." Here, we can see another display of human potential: "His mannerism did not allude to the gravity of what was about to take place at all." This suggests Saigō' had an amazing tanryoku, or a great deal of courage.

Possessing tanryoku means to have kikotsu, or a strong backbone, and kiryoku-kotsuryoku, or vitality and vigor. Kiryoku is a life force energy that arises from tanden, which refers to the human body's center of gravity located in the lower abdominal area below the navel. Kotsuryoku, the workings of bone marrow and blood stream, represents ardency and volition. When cultivating kiryoku-kotsuryoku, what becomes most important is ritsuyō, or to straighten one's back. Having a straight posture has two benefits. First, the straight back helps the blood in the bone marrow to circulate more efficiently. Second, keeping a straight posture allows the lower abdomen to slightly expand which helps to smooth out the intestinal peristaltic activity and increase energy. The basis of human potential is to remain calm and self-possessed even when confronted with a grave matter.

Back to the Saigō and Katsu's negotiations. Katsu also recalled: "As the negotiation proceeded, Saigō trusted every word I said and did not raise even a trace of doubt. He simply said 'it will be very difficult to persuade my army, but I will do anything I can do to deal with the situation.' His words saved tens of thousands of lives as well as properties in Edo, and shogun Tokugawa was spared defeat." This account illustrates the power and preciousness of one's words. What Saigō's words – "I will do anything I can do to deal with the situation" – were able to save was undoubtedly immense. Whether we could bring ourselves to say the last words, words of conclusion, epitomizes our human potential.

What brought Saigō to say those words? First, he had trust in Katsu, having risked his own life by choosing to try to negotiate with Saigō. He knew it was important for him to sincerely acknowledge this fact. Second, he deeply understood the very difficult decision Katsu had to make in accepting the undesirable role at a time of crisis. Lastly, being the one with the upper hand, Saigō felt the need to extend compassion and sensitivity toward the other side. These factors all contributed to his remarks.

This awareness of Saigo's can be summarized as "jin-gi-rei-chi-shin" – benevolence, righteousness, ritual, wisdom and integrity. His awareness was exactly what these five virtues are. He had a heart to be considerate of others. We can also say that he had a heart to respect and value the lives of others. Saigō was fully aware that if he had said "no" to Katsu's proposal, Katsu would have taken his own life right then and there. He was able to recognize this because he had always put himself in the place of others. Jin-gi-rei-chi-shin is, as mentioned in the book Bushido: The Soul of Japan written by Nitobe Inazō, the foundation of human potential.

There was another thing Saigō had to be concerned about. By then, the members of imperial forces had lost many of their close family members through hard and fierce battles. Surely they had strong resentment after suffering through years of the shogunate's tyranny. Therefore, it was completely uncertain whether his men would willingly obey the terms Saigō had accepted with Katsu. Besides, they were approaching very close to the enemy's base, Edo castle. A perfect opportunity to avenge themselves was almost in their hands. Nevertheless, Saigō was about to call the battle off. That is why his words – "I will do anything I can do to deal with the situation" – carried huge weight. He understood the circumstances very well and, above all, he had complete trust in his people. Or, at least, he was confident with his relationships with them. He had amazing faith in them. His words, therefore, were meant for himself and his men as much as they were meant for Katsu.

## 2-15 IN-EN-KA: THE FUNDAMENTALS OF PERSONAL RELATIONSHIPS

One of the problems modern society is faced with is the rapid increase of young people who have difficulty relating to others. Clearly, this is a very serious problem. For human beings, to grow is to deepen our sociality. Eventually, everyone matures and becomes full members of society.

What is society? It is a community that is comprised of ourselves as individuals and everyone else. Therefore, becoming a full member of society depends on how well we could build a personal relationship with other people. Particularly, places like corporations are typical examples that provide great opportunities to interact with people from different walks of life. Only after establishing good relationships with these individuals, will we be able to fully perform our work. Otherwise, we are not considered as a full-fledged member of society; therefore, an increase of such individuals indicates society is on a path to an unsustainable future.

What contributes to this phenomenon? Numerous speculations have been raised yet most of them point to the sparseness of direct experience of diverse personal relationships. Because people have completely unique personalities, their views and opinions are largely different from each other's. People have different taste. There are some we dislike or find rather annoying. There are plenty of rude and violent individuals as well. Yet, better relationships are built on actual experiences of these encounters.

This involves occasional face-to-face confrontations with one another, even hurting each other at times, and losing faith in fellow human beings once in awhile. These are all part of growing up, but such experiences have become scarce lately. Why is this the case? Many point to the fact that young people's interactions have been limited to video games and their communications with others to emails and cell phones since they were little. But I sense something larger is contributing to this problem.

In Buddhism, there is a concept of 'engi, or codependent origination, of the mutual containment and interpenetration of all phenomena.' One thing contains all things in existence while all things contain one; therefore, one may be an independent being but one is not self-existent in an absolute sense. This means that all things and phenomena – interrelated and inexhaustible – in this world affect our existence. This thought was based on the philosophy of the inseparability of self and others which assumes that no one is completely isolated from other people.

First of all, we are here today as a result of a very long historical line of descent involving a great number of people. We were born to our parents, but when tracing back our lineage further generations to our parents' parents and their parents and so on, we realize that it took tens of thousands of people existing before us for us to be here today. We are the fruits of these unions. Besides, hands of others many times over have been lent to us to make our existence possible. Because it would have been entirely possible for an entire family to perish from crude living conditions or disasters, our presence is a true testament to fortunate blessings. Our existence, therefore, is the manifestation of the perfect interlinking of various events and factors. We were born and given a life as a result of the causation.

There are two kinds of such causation in the Buddhist belief: "In," a direct cause, and "en," a contributory cause. Combine the two, and we have "in-nen," or direct and indirect causes. The concept of in-nen further evolved into the idea of "engi," or codependent origination. This is based on a belief that all phenomena in this world – from human kind to animals and even our anguish – exists due to the effect of various in-nen interconnecting with one another. Nothing exists independently without such interrelations. Consequently, without cause

# Chapter 2 • Exploring Management Approaches Of The East / 59

and conditions, there will naturally be no "ka," a result. Therefore, 'engi of the mutual containment and interpenetration of all phenomena' describes the idea that there is absolutely nothing in the entire world that does not affect each of our beings, that everything is infinitely codependent.

Western thought, on the other hand, tends to view things more objectively by separating self from others or situations. Or, putting it rather directly, it highly values the building of self that is completely independent of others. During modern times, Japan had vigorously adopted such Western concepts, and even more distinct Western egotism became accentuated after the war. In addition, mixed with the culture of competitive society, the tendency to outdo others at any cost grew even stronger, resulting with individuals who seemingly regard everyone else as their competition.

In Western society, such extreme individualism is redressed by Catholic moral values so as not to go out of control. However, with no such resistant in place, Japan has regrettably created self-serving and self-centered individuals who suffer from social withdrawal or seal themselves off from society. We must immediately put a stop to this grave situation.

What could help remedy this situation tremendously is the aforementioned 'engi of the mutual containment and interpenetration of all phenomena.' Founded on the belief that no one is unconnected from others, it shows 'there is no self without others.' It teaches us not only to value the existence of others, but also to appreciate the fact that their existence is what sustains our own lives. There will never be a climate in which people heedlessly take lives of others in a society that builds on this idea.

## 2-16 CO-CREATION AND COEXISTENCE: THE 21ST CENTURY BUSINESS MODEL

Today, businesses face a need to change themselves. It is over six decades since the war ended. They need a fundamental transformation. Situations surrounding businesses have changed drastically – management resources, for instance.

First of all, in terms of personnel, outdated human resources departments – whose main functions consist of handling individuals as labor based on a so-called workforce management system, placing them to fill vacant positions systematically according to a flexible organization chart and undertaking recruitment and staffing on an as needed basis – do not exist anymore. And implementations of employment contracts based on portal-to-portal pay have eliminated the need for the kind of management practices that enforce strict business hours. What is demanded of workers is quality. Now workers are required to deliver more than their assumed responsibilities with qualities surpassing a certain level through applying highly specialized skills. The tasks of human resources departments have shifted to securing workforces that can meet such demand and to providing an environment where workers can fully realize their potential.

In terms of goods and money, the kinds of information and knowledge they embody are considered much more important than what they actually represent. Businesses have become more drawn to and recognize values in accumulation of knowledge such as business models that guarantee to generate steady and assured sales for the coming years, even more so than earning a temporary surge of financial gain or generating amazing sales off of a single successful product. Quality is being demanded here as well.

Also a dynamic shift is sought in businesses' relationships with their customers. The market once was a place where exchanges of values – between sellers' products and buyers' money – took place and where the interactions of the two sides were very candid, taking place only at the moment of exchange. But it is different now. Businesses' approaches have shifted more toward developing products that could entice buyers to willingly and actively engage in such exchanges and building lasting relationships of mutual trust with them. Consequently, businesses have to have a deeper understanding of desires and needs of their customers, requiring that both sides communicate with each other at a more profound level. Having strong and close relationships with customers have become more important than ever.

In other words, having lasting life-partner-like relationships based on mutual trust and symbiotic and uniting relationships where both sellers and buyers stand on the same side has become essential. As these shifts suggest, companies are now confronted with the demands for adopting completely new dimensions, both inside and outside. And looking into elements of the new dimensions reveals the concept of "co-creation and coexistence."

Co-creation refers to acts of creation where people with unique personalities come together united by common goals to express their creativities and create results that are far better than anyone could anticipate through dramatic advances only made possible by their diversity.

Coexistence refers to where people with different and opposing points of views live together as an indispensible presence to one another by establishing mutually complementary relationships based upon mutual acceptance.

What these two have in common is that, first of all, people who engage in them are established as individuals. Therefore, they already express and assert their original distinctiveness. Naturally, there are times when these individuals may clash with one another. But at the same time they are held together by underlying mutual acceptance, and because of this, they know they can anticipate achieving dramatic and unexpected results. And that is why they decidedly need one another.

Until recently, most things were headed in opposite directions. In any organization, because showing too much individuality was thought to create discord with others, individuals repressed their personal opinions and engaged in work with great emphasis on cooperation. This contributed to smooth workplace relationships. However, since these organizations were, after all, a group of homogeneous individuals trying to create something new, outcomes rarely reached beyond expectations. The workers' creativity often did not go beyond identifying weakness in competitors' products and tweaking them just enough to market them as their own. No astounding and innovative, passionate and ambitious products could come out of such an environment. In order to ensure Japanese companies' continuing global success going forward, they need to focus on creating organizations that are based on the ideas of co-creation and coexistence.

The key is this: Don't be afraid of things that are fundamentally different. Japanese workers tended to dislike people who expressed different opinions from theirs and even excluded such individuals. They welcomed an organization that was composed only of like-minded individuals, considering it as a "good company." Such organization could be a comfortable place to be for some, but we cannot expect something revolutionary to emerge from such a tepid environment. At best, what could come out of this culture are businesses that are terribly less competitive and more bureaucratic.

In order to avoid such a foolish path, businesses need to have a firm, unwavering philosophical background. What kind of ideology should be behind the idea of co-creation and coexistence? The philosophies of Mahayana, "great vehicle," Buddhism. Its thoughts contrast with Hinayana, "inferior vehicle," Buddhism which believes people have to renounce the world in order to achieve enlightenment. Mahayana Buddhism, on the other hand, does not disfavor monks nor lay people, but instead it believes everyone can achieve anuttara samyaksambodhi, or 'unexcelled complete enlightenment,' as Buddha has.

Therefore, we can all coexist if we can overcome differences – positions, circumstances, nationalities and ethnicities – and share a common goal to come to our senses and desire to achieve enlightenment. In fact, we are already here in this world at the same time and era to do this very thing – exist together. This is a belief passed down from generations to generations throughout communities in Japan.

## 2-17 LEARNING WORK ETHICS FROM SHŌSAN SUZUKI

Today, a change is also sought in the relationships between a business and its employees. It is because the "meaning of work" is being questioned again. This is epitomized by the growing social issues concerning the sharp increase of people who lack full time employment or are unemployed. These people chose not to seek the full-time employment of a particular company. Although various reasons and circumstances probably led them to where they are, what seems to be behind their surge is the public distrust of businesses.

A spate of scandals involving businesses has continually been making headlines. Most of these are antisocial, inhumane misdeeds committed solely to put profits ahead of everything else. It should not surprise us at all if young people, with their incorrupt minds still intact, despise becoming members of such organizations. Besides, if they had to witness their parents, having been caught in the recent whirlwind of corporate restructuring, become targets of workforce reductions and let go from their jobs so thoughtlessly, it is no wonder they question the value of employment. Now, more than six decades since the end of the war, Japanese businesses are finally at a major turning point.

What is called into question is "why people work." How far in the fundamental principles do we need to revert to in order to find an answer? We need to turn to the teaching of a Zen priest of the Edo period, Shōsan Suzuki. He is widely known for having greatly influenced establishing the work ethics of Japanese people which have been passed down for many generations.

We need to turn to his teachings, because this is the origin of Japanese businesses.

What Shōsan taught was, in short, "the affairs of this world are the teachings of Buddha and the teachings of Buddha are the affairs of this world" – the teachings of Buddha can be found in everyday life. Regardless of the type of job one has, if one devotes oneself fully, it becomes the same as participating in Buddhist practices. Let us look closely at the details of his teachings.

First, there are commonalities between the era Shōsan lived and the one we live today. During his time, Japan finally saw an end to the Warring States period and the feudal system under the Tokugawa clan began to take shape. Peace had been restored at last to the nation. There was a significant shift underway – the nation was about to shift from the government which ruled by force to a civilian government. It was a major turning point in the nation's history, a situation which we also find ourselves in today.

Furthermore, during the time of relative peace – both then and now – feelings of tension typically dissipate from the public, and people are likely to see little importance in the pursuit of spirituality. It is also the time where peace is often taken for granted as people seek only immediate gratifications and ethical values are sparse. In these ways, ours and Shōsan's time seem similar.

Originally, Shōsan served the Tokugawa family as a samurai and fought in a series of major battles including the Battle of Sekigahara and the winter and summer campaigns of the siege of Osaka. But at the age of twenty-four he renounced the world to live the life of a Buddhist. His decision to become a monk did not arise from the common desires at the time to escape from reality – such as out of despair of loss of life or harboring discontent with the life as a samurai. Rather, he chose the path with the hopes to reform the corrupt and confused state of the nation. After years of strict and relentless training, he established his own school of thought at the age of fifty-five and devoted his entire life offering salvation to ordinary people until his death at seventy-seven.

The premise of Shōsan's teaching was "equality." He made clear that regardless of where one is from, everyone is equal when it comes to achieving enlightenment. From this belief, the idea of "shimin-byōdō," or the equality of shimin, the four social classes, emerged. In his book Shimin-nichiyō, Shōsan writes that shimin represents the four classes – samurais, farmers, artisans and merchants – and nichiyō refers to using something every day or keeping something in mind at all times. He, then, goes on to explain nichiyō for each class.

In Bushi-nichiyō for samurais, he writes that because the primary duty of a samurai is to govern the nation, fulfilling one's duty courageously and impregnably equates to the undertaking of the training to attain Buddhahood. In Nōmin-nichiyō for farmers, he writes that farming is itself a Buddhist activity. Reciting Namu-aminda-butsu, every movement of the hoe equates to the undertaking of the training to attain Buddhahood. In Shokunin-nichiyō, for artisans, he writes that working is itself a Buddhist activity. Pray to attain Buddhahood and believe in the self. Believe in the self means to carry out one's work while believing that Buddha is found within one's self, therefore the act itself is to believe the heart of the Buddha. Working with such a mind equates to the undertaking of the training to attain Buddhahood. In Shōnin-nichiyō for merchants, he writes that earnestly honing integrity and dedicating oneself completely to the way of heaven to provide the nation with an abundant supply of commodities equates to the undertaking of the training to attain Buddhahood.

Essentially, Shōsan taught that performing one's work assiduously and wholeheartedly at all times itself is considered the same as partaking in Buddhist practices. And doing so would lead to "muge-daijizai," or complete freedom from all obstacles, thus becoming enlightened. We work because it rewards us. We work to achieve a sense of peace and joyful lives. This inner peace comes from engaging in one's task with devotion as if it is a Buddhist practice. And doing so can also lead to improving the lives of others. Labor itself is a Buddhist activity; therefore, it leads us to salvation. This idea has evolved into what we recognize today as the traditional Japanese work ethics which is based on the cycle of three elements: Labor, Buddhist activity and salvation. And what is remarkable is that it also encompasses the concept of professional ethics.

What makes the teachings of Shōsan Suzuki so admirable is that they are not some didactic set of lofty ideals from high above, but rather they are easily understood and practical. This is best illustrated by what he taught one has to do before engaging in any work: 'Cultivate the proper mind.' Shōsan believed that, first and foremost, it is very important to properly prepare one's mind prior to engaging in anything. And this involves taming the three poisons that exist within: Greed, anger and discontent. Greed is to be carried away with inappropriate desire. Anger is to get upset when one cannot have one's way. Discontent is to focus too much on things that are absent and lose the feeling of gratitude. Shōsan Suzuki taught that the starting point is to be in control of these three poisons.

## 2-18 MANAGEMENT BASED ON "SELF-BENEFIT FOR THE BENEFIT OF OTHERS"

*It* appears that many corporations continue to be rife with problems and immersed in a state of disorder. Most of the problems are often related to their relation with society. If I may expostulate a little, Japanese corporations have been overly possessed with the idea that anything is accomplishable within themselves. And they are under the illusion that they are completely independent from the society in which they exist.

As mergers, acquisitions and hostile takeovers frequent the recent headlines, I cannot help but imagine most of the targeted businesses never dreamed it happening to them. In fact, in most cases, such dealings are initiated by people with no prior connection to the involved businesses, often located faraway. Corporations have become global entities exposing themselves to a great number of people worldwide. That means the rights to be their customers or even stockholders have been extended practically to anyone.

Japanese corporations have been guarded by a stable network of stockholders. Cross shareholding by financial institutions and group companies have been common practice. However, this strong solidarity has resulted in the severing of information flow and the breeding of a self-righteous, autocratic management style. For those organizations that are more or less in the same boat, what kind of management philosophy should they adopt as their new foundation?

In the Buddhist belief, there is a concept of "jiri-soku-rita," or self-benefit for the benefit of others. This could be a little hard to grasp today as people tend to process things in dualistic terms and operate with "either-or" thinking. But, its basic principle is quite simple. When both sides are chosen together, they both subsist, but when only one of them is chosen, they both lose. In other words, we benefit only if we provide benefits to others. Moreover, we do things for the others' benefit because we know we will gain as much from it in turn. The point is self-benefit and others' benefit are one and the same. They are considered inseparable.

Conversely, neither working solely to benefit the self nor working solely to benefit others can be sustained. Both efforts often complement each other and maximize the outcome with synergistic effect. For instance, let's say we do something only for our satisfaction and the money we can bring in for ourselves. What we get as the result of this will always be the same story. When faced with great difficulties or obstacles, we will not be able to tap into the incredible abilities we innately have or the kind of superhuman strength people summon in emergencies. We simply cannot use them if the purpose is to only enrich ourselves.

In terms of our immediate surroundings, desires to take care of our parents who have tirelessly cared and supported us can draw this ability. Even in a case of groundbreaking research and development, the energy to ultimately make the breakthrough possible arises from a sense of responsibility to one's colleagues or the company. A sense of urgency – the result of one's work determines the future of the company, for instance – could also bring out this power.

What this means is that only through serving others, can we finally fulfill our potential as human beings. This is how we bring well-being and make meaningful contributions to our colleagues, the companies we work for and even society. Then, we will receive everything we did in return. First, we become fulfilled with the feeling of contentment for bringing joy to others. Then, we are rewarded by the appreciation from the company and pay increases in recognition of our contributions. Furthermore, we receive further praise and appreciation from society, consequently increasing the revenue for the business.

In the case of workers, they work by pushing themselves harder to the brink hoping to serve their family, friends, colleagues and company. What the company needs to do is to provide this opportunity to their workers and show them how rare it is. Then, to add some pressure, which is also an important element, set a deadline and immerse them completely in given tasks. When they hit a wall, have them work as a team to solve the problem. Make sure everyone in the company, including the very top members, are encouraging and motivating their workers throughout the process.

When they finally overcome the obstacle and achieve the goal, applaud their hard work and recognize their contributions. The details about the outcome of a product release and the results of the workers' devotion should be shared with the people involved. Such details include how the products are received and valued by consumers and how that translates into the company's overall performance. If the achievement is truly remarkable from a global standpoint, that means the company has made a contribution to the nation, making it the recipient of subsequent national recognition. This ultimate "act for the benefit of others" – prospering not only the business but also society, the nation and even the world – is going to be returned to each contributor as "self-benefit."

Before going global or even national, there is a worker, a single human being, at every base point. But the businesses' reach is indeed at a global level. Instead of directly returning to the workers, profits are passed down along many people who have some level of involvement. This is the nature of how corporations operate. According to Buddhist beliefs, human society in which corporations exist is a community based on the spirit of "self-benefit for the benefit of others."

This brings us to the question of to whom do corporations belong. We could say they belong to each employee or all the individuals who contribute to the business, in some way, rather than the persisting notion that corporations belong to the self-righteous owner who is responsible for the devising of boisterous acquisitions and hostile takeovers. Connected at the global level, these contributors are united by the relationship based on "resonance and unity." At first, they are customers, and then some of them become employees or shareholders of a company. Adopting this concept of "self-benefit for the benefit of others" at the foundation of business may represent the future of corporations.

## 2-19 A NEW MODEL FOR CORPORATIONS ACCORDING TO HŌNEN SHONIN

As we move forward in the twenty-first century, businesses are confronted with the urgent need to fundamentally reform themselves. This call to change indicates the difficulty of envisioning businesses – whose only offer is a makeshift solution spun out of the concepts and ideas steeped in Western scientific thought – as truly indispensible and beneficial entities for society and the public.

Hōnen Shonin, the founder of Jōdo Buddhism, once said: "Live fully by devoting to nembutsu, or Buddhist chants, entrusting where they guide us and recite them with determination." According to him, we are here to seek inner peace. Our ultimate goal is to lead a life with the state of unequivocal impregnable placidity. Worldly desires such as wealth and fame should not be denied. But they are not the ultimate goal in life because such desires know no limits. With their boundless greed, desires will continue to demand for more. In other words, no definitive feeling of satisfaction comes from pursuit of worldly desires. Such pursuit will constantly bring the lingering feeling of discontent. It is far from the state of permanence, a state of inner peace.

Furthermore, Hōnen also said that in order to attain the "state of nembutsu," it does not matter whether one renounces the world to pursue the Buddhist training or continues on one's life as a lay person. What matters is arriving at this state. He stated a clear relationship between the purpose in life and the work one has. Work provides a pathway to reach enlightenment. It does not matter what occupation one chooses. One should do whatever one wishes. The most important thing is whether one has something to pursue day after day through one's work, or has a clear objective in life that one strives to achieve. According to Hōnen, the meaning of life depends on whether one has these things. In other words, a great job is not what we need to seek; rather, we need to seek the spiritual state which we can acquire through performing a job. Not a type of career or a company we work for, but attaining a desirable inner spiritual state should be the goal in life.

In postwar Japan, people focused on bringing security and stability to their lives, or most fundamentally, having something to eat. Although Japan is now a major economic powerhouse and its citizens enjoy wealth and prosperity, this mindset and aspiration of working for food security is still instilled as a principle in Japanese people. A problem is that despite the fact the nation is well beyond the point where getting something to eat should dominate the reason to work, it has not yet found a new objective to replace it.

What perfectly illustrates this is what we see on TV. Purportedly, TV programs mirror the state of the nation, reflecting the mood and desires of the general public. What seem to dominate Japan's airtime are shows about gourmet food in which someone is always eating something. Another regular is shows featuring multimillionaires flaunting their extravagant lifestyles or people who are sadly blinded by luxury brands, shopping away. This trend indicates that the center of our drive is still about putting food on the table – only more lavish and extravagant. It is the same for the desires to be rich and accumulate wealth – just with even more money and possessions. These are all materialistic aspirations. No matter how far we pursue them, they will never be anything more than materialistic goals. What all this amounts to is an endless relative comparison about who has more.

What is asked of us is to find a new goal to replace the old now that the materialistic goals have been well satisfied. In other words, we are in urgent need to shift the entire spectrum of the meaning of life itself. A materialistic goal has a certain importance, but we are at a point where we have to embrace a clear spiritual goal with the same enthusiasm and volition. When we grasp this notion, we can feel the words of Hōnen Shonin slowly sinking into our mind: "Live fully by devoting to nembutsu chants, entrusting where they guide us and reciting them with determination."

Not surprisingly, businesses are also asked to make similar changes. First, they need to rethink whether their unequivocal focus on chasing materialistic objectives such as sales figures and profit margins is working for them. These financial figures do provide a useful and necessary yardstick to keep track of the states of their business operations. But today, businesses are asked to reflect on whether they make contributions to society in truly beneficial and indispensable ways, and whether they provide the best place for their workers to perform their tasks and spend their valuable time.

Many people point out the potential businesses have as spiritual training grounds. Through a variety of settings, work presents us with growth opportunities. We need to be more aware of these positive sides of businesses, intentionally bring them out, attentively recreate and magnify them. Needless to say, when workers grow as persons through mental discipline, not only the companies but society as a whole also benefits.

Through working assiduously and wholeheartedly, workers enter a state of complete self-effacement. They become grateful to their colleagues who struggled together to overcome hurdles and challenges, and even become astonished by their greatness and excellence as individuals. Through negotiating and dealing with customers and vendors, workers learn to give their absolute best. They even become moved by the realization that there is no separation between them and others. According to Hōnen Shonin, businesses need to be a place where workers can actually feel and experience these things and enrich themselves to achieve spiritual gratification.

## 2-20 LEARNING A CUSTOMER-DRIVEN BUSINESS PRACTICE FROM ZEN

When imagining the future of business management, what becomes clear is the importance of customer relationships. An ideal relationship is, to put it simply, the one established on a "mutually sympathetic and empathetic connection." First, both sides have to be willing to build a true partnership and overcome the hierarchical relations of who has an upper hand. A business is only successful if it has become truly indispensible to its customers. In order to win them over, businesses have to begin with mind preparation.

Buddhist teachings offer a perfect approach: "Jita-funi." This means self and others are one, there is no self without others and there are no others without the self. Essentially, there is no concept of separating sellers from buyers at its basis. In order to satisfy and make the best of one's self, one must satisfy and make the best of others. But because needs have a tendency to intensify, simply uniting sellers and buyers does not offer enough satisfaction to either side. What is it, then, that it required?

What buyers demand from sellers is, first of all, the professional quality that transcends the individuals – nonprofessionals. In Japan, such quality has been known for ages as "kurōto." Kuro means black or darkness. Therefore, a kurōto refers to a person who has the ability to see in the dark. What does the dark refer to? The minds of customers.

There is a Chinese character "意" (pronounced i:). It means the sound of the mind. To listen to an unvoiced mind is "to communicate the sound of the mind." First, sellers are required to communicate with buyers or customers at this level and identify their unspoken desires. Then, the sellers have to turn the desires of the customers into reality. This is made possible by the sellers' or kurōtos' exceptional knowledge, skills and, especially, sensitivities – all of which are intangible. In other words, for businesses to be able to communicate with customers at the unseen and inaudible level will become important for the coming consumer driven market.

To understand how we can apply this concept, we now turn to Zen. The origin of Zen Buddhism is ascribed to "Nengemishō," or, the Flower Sermon. One day, Gautama Siddhārtha Buddha gathered people around him on the Griddhraj Parvat Hill and told them he was going to deliver a special sermon today. The followers silently anticipated for him to begin. Moments later he finally picked a lotus flower beside him and held it for all to see. While the followers were perplexed with what was unfolding in front of their eyes, his leading disciple Mahākā☒yapa put a big smile on his face as he watched what Gautama Siddhārtha Buddha was doing. The Gotama Siddhattha Buddha then said: "I possess the true Dharma eye, the marvelous mind of Nirvana, the true form of the formless, the subtle Dharma gate that does not rest on words or letters but is a special transmission outside of the scriptures. This I entrust to Mahākā☒yapa." What this story shows us is that the teachings of Zen cannot be conveyed in words or even in the Buddhist scriptures. It is not something that can be taught.

Accompanying this anecdote, there is a well-known phrase, "Ishin-denshin," or communicating with another mind-to-mind without expressing the message in words. Looking deeper into the meaning of this phrase, first, we notice a common foundation between the two people who successfully communicate in this way; both of them are working toward a mutual goal. Then, we realize that they are seeking things that cannot be written or spoken. In other words, they are seeking things that can only be realized through actual shared experiences. And this can only be communicated by looking into each other's eyes and exchanging smiles as their minds align perfectly.

Businesses' relationships with customers also have to continue to evolve as well. To do this, businesses will begin by streamlining the level of service through implementing a company-wide operations manual. Over time, their relationship with their customers will reach a level of sophistication, precisely the level of "ishin-denshin." Once this is reached, what should they do to sustain this level? The more sophisticated the business-client relationship becomes, the more difficult the training of successors becomes. Even in a situation like this, Zen teachings offer us great practical guidance.

What method has Zen practice adopted in order to pass down the truth and spiritual awakening that are utterly inexplicable in words? Its essence is summarized in the phrase, "jikishi-ninshin," which means to point directly at the human mind. For example, imagine a teacher and a disciple deeply engaging in work or a task together. At the moment that they become fully immersed in what they are doing and completely free from obstructive thoughts, their minds unite and become one. If the disciple unexpectedly performs, in this circumstance, even a part of the techniques intended to be passed down to him or her, what needs to happen is for the teacher to quickly recognize and simply point to it by saying, "there, that was it!" This is what jikishi-ninshin is.

Aside from acquired techniques, abilities such as performing subtle adjustments involve the state of mind and the level of emotion one is in at the moment. These things are incommunicable by mere words. All one can do is to let others try, point out when they get it right and make sure they commit it into their memory. Such communication is at a level attainable only by utilizing abilities unique to humans. And, this is what will be essential for business activities from now on.

## 2-21 TRANSFORMING BUSINESS WITH TAOISM

As we move forward in the twenty-first century, we began to see some aspects of the new century. Where a shift is most apparent is in the way of businesses and the environment surrounding them. One example is a disparity between the increasing sophistication of the values companies offer to consumers and the conditions within the organizations where such values are created.

Today's consumers are no longer satisfied with an industry-standard product and service nor do they accept it as something of value. In other words, businesses can no longer count on such products and service to drive their performance. That is why they devote everything they have to create far better values than their competitors could match, and by doing so, outdo their rivals.

Essentially, what companies offer to the public is the fruit of their dreams-turned-reality. But in actuality, workers behind these products are often distressed. This gap is what is at issue. Besides, it appears as though there is no clear end in sight to this competitive climate. Recognizing such uncertainty, some workers quite naturally question whether they want to continue to endure such straining working conditions and eventually decide to quit their jobs.

The younger workforce has already been declining. Businesses will have to do more to attract and secure as many good talents as they can. Therefore this inconsistency between increasing the sophistication of the values companies offer and their internal rifts must be resolved no matter what. It is inevitable that consumers' needs will only become more sophisticated over time.

On a closer look, we realize that this issue actually consists of compounding problems. First, it is a problem of competition and rivalry among business competitors. Second, it is a problem of the nature of businesses where a qualitative demand such as sophistication is treated only as a quantitative need. Lastly, it is a problem of companies' internal systems where companies try to systematically handle such qualitative demands by setting quotas for their workers. In short, the issue stems from trying to deal with a new demand – to produce and provide the company's original value – with an outdated management philosophy and system that idealizes producing as much as possible and as effectively as possible, out of limited resources. Businesses today are strongly asked to change their way of thinking.

As we have noted earlier, the word Tao in Taoism, the philosophy of Lao-tzu and Chuang-tzu, refers to "the way," the origin of the world. According to Tao, the world consists of heaven, earth, all creations – animals, plants, minerals among others – and qi, or vital energy, which includes air. The world is where all of these things freely engage in what they are meant to do and interact with one another harmoniously. All of their creators, or mothers, are "the way." In addition, "the way" never stops giving life to even more new things. "Creation and evolution," which this working of "the way" is called, is the true essence of the profound workings of "the way." Therefore, the essence of the world we live in lies within creativeness that is unceasingly brought to life day after day.

All creations brought to the world do not remain the same as they first appear. They continue to grow, change and reproduce. All creations are interrelated, and they exist and act in mutual, coordinated relationships with one another. That means "the way" is rather coordinated, not unorganized or mechanical, and rather diverse and dynamic, not prosaic or monotonous. Its special quality is its creative dynamism.

Although the way has created so many incredibly valuable things, it never asks anything in return. It appears that because it receives great pleasure from bringing forth all things to the world and satisfaction as though doing so fulfills its purpose, its creative energy and power never become exhausted nor does it ever get tired. It is as if "the way" turns such gratification and joy into the source of its energy and power.

To learn from this nature of "the way" and to live one's life following it is called the way of virtue. When this nature of "the way" is expressed through a person, it is called virtue. "The way of virtue," therefore, is something very dynamic and energetic.

Eastern philosophy, especially that of Lao-tze and Chuang-tze, shares an idea that to live in harmony and conformity with heaven, earth and nature is to assimilate with "the way." And our vitality is retained in its most natural way if we live accordingly. In other words, in Eastern philosophy, to unite and coexist with "the way" – or heaven, earth and nature – is to unite and coexist with all things "the way" created. And we unite with the order of the universe by doing so.

In Western philosophy, on the other hand, it seems as though nature is considered something to be subdued, and an idea about how to separate nature from us and build a competitive relationship between the two is much emphasized. It is this Western thinking that today's businesses are based upon.

Therefore, looking at them from a Taoist perspective, I sense a big problem in their current state. What I strongly think, most of all, is that their organizational structures seem too unnatural. It seems like it could be more of a spontaneous and open-minded environment where people gather naturally. Moreover, heaven, earth and nature mean society, thus businesses have to establish a more harmonious and coexisting relationship with it.

Another thing I notice is an undesirable situation people in these businesses, their workers, are in. For us, an act of creation itself is a fundamental vital activity. It is clear from the creative activities of the world's renowned artists that unless what we do is rooted in a fundamental vital activity, we cannot engage in a true creative activity. In other words, joy of life comes from engaging in creative activities. They are what we can completely absorb and selflessly devote ourselves to, and doing so is to unite with heaven, earth and nature.

Artists embrace new challenges because they know they will experience an ultimate joy through engaging in a creative activity. It is very important for businesses to realize that anyone should be able to approach their work with a desire to embody their dreams, and a company is a collective entity of such desires.

## 2-22  LEARNING EMPLOYEE-COMPANY RELATIONSHIPS FROM DŌGEN ZENJI

When we think of the future of corporations, what appears as problematic is the relationship between "individuals and the whole." Establishing a renewed relationship between individuals – workers – and the whole – companies – becomes the basis. The businesses have definitely dominated in this relationship dynamics while individual workers have accounted for very little. The conventions have been that workers are pushed around by the companies because workers would not have existed without the companies to offer them jobs. Without a place to work, they would have no way of expressing their abilities. But, the situation has changed drastically.

Customers' needs have shifted from products that can make up for what is lacking to products that can fulfill their emotional needs. When catering to such desire, simply improving productivity or enduring physical labor changes nothing. What needs to improve is "intellectual productivity." What companies demand from their employees, therefore, is to create values no one else has from their accumulated "knowledge." For the workers, this shift presents a great opportunity. They could make an amazing impact by presenting business ideas or business models that could actually improve companies' overall performance. An era where workers and companies – individuals and the whole – are at equals has arrived.

There is a concept known as 'en' in the Buddhist belief. According to en, each of us does not exist alone. As long as we live, we have to have some kind of relationship with other people. In other words, no one can survive if not for the connections to others. Others in this sense are not limited to people. As described in "san-sen-sou-boku-shitsuu-bussyō" (mountain, river, grass and trees all have Buddha nature) or "sou-boku-kokudo-shikkai-jobutsu" (grass, tree and land all become Buddha), everything in this world is believed to have the same Buddha nature as humans. Basically, based on these concepts, each of us is inseparable from everything that exists in this world.

Because of the existence of the great universe as a whole, I as an individual exist. Since I also inherently has a small universe within, I and the macrocosm have an equivalent relationship. As to prove this, we all have individuality. Each of us unequivocally leads a unique existence. Why? It is because we are microcosms comprised of complete independence and originality. This, according to the Buddhist ideas, perfectly illustrates the fundamental relationship between individuals and the whole. This also means that the long-held idea where the workers are subordinate to their employer is contrived whereas an equal relationship of the two, being sought now, is the way it should be.

Given all of this, what workers are asked of now is to strengthen their autonomy, independence and individuality. They also need to improve and express their "knowledge" – namely the know-how, techniques and experience they have acquired. What kind of lifestyle do they need to adopt in order to achieve these? Here are the words of Dōgen Zenji, a prominent Japanese Buddhist thinker and the founder of the Sōtō school of Zen. "Shōya-zen-kigen, shiya-zen-kigen" Live fully and depart fully. Live out one's life profoundly and deliberately until the last breath – that is, according to Dōgen Zenji, what it means to live a better life.

We live in the passage of time. Time and our lives exist in a relationship in which both flow from one moment to the next. Both experiences repeat over and over as the future becomes now and now becomes the past. What is important is that we cannot grasp the future or the past. We can only grasp "right now." Once "now" passes, everything becomes the past. Time waits for no one. Just as water escapes from cupped hands, time flows down to the past relentlessly. "Now" is, needless to say, incontrovertibly precious. But, we are guilty of occasionally letting it merely pass by, for instance, sleeping away. There is nothing more wasteful than that. What Dōgen Zenji would say to this is if we are going to sleep, do so to the heart's content. In addition, he would certainly disapprove of time-wasting, unnecessary meetings where participants are bored, agonized and simply counting down the minutes until they are over. He asks us whether we are living this very moment to the utter fullest as the basis of how we spent our time.

Another point is: We will never get the past back. There is nothing we can do about the time called past. But let's be honest. We all have had a remarkable amount of time consumed for the things that have already happened. What occupies our mind for the most of the time is apparently about what we have done or said before. We have to ask ourselves whether it is really worth spending the very precious moment, now, for something we cannot change. Dōgen Zenji advises us to live in the moment while putting the past completely behind while always looking straight into the future.

One another point is: The progress of time means the arrival of a brand new "now. Human cells are said to constantly regenerate themselves. To look at the future while living in the moment also represents amazing creativity. To keep embracing new challenges and striving to create – the act that is innately human – is where our true joy lies and how we can always feel a connection with the greater universe.

## 2-23 THE ESSENCE OF LEADERSHIP

A basic principle of classical Chinese philosophy is "human salvation lies only in the hands of humans." The ancient Chinese stopped relying on gods and Buddha for their needs. Instead, they established a realistic approach where they sought fellow humans for betterment. They came to the conclusion that human happiness, after all, depends on the worthiness of their leader. The question, then, became how to cultivate a leader. They thought they could not simply hope for a great leader to appear by luck because government and political systems exist for the happiness of its citizens. It was simply too risky to leave the rise of a leader, who has the authority to run them, up to chance.

This led to an exploration on finding ways to intentionally create a great leader. What came of it is the Four Books and Five Classics – a curriculum designed for fostering human resources. These Chinese classics are thus textbooks for human resource development. A philosophy and an education system, they were textbooks for leadership development – probably nothing comes close to the level of their quality and sophistication. Fully integrated with Japan's unique traditional spiritual culture, this education system became the foundation of the Edo period, lasting some three hundred years. It is quite shocking that such a qualitatively and quantitatively effective system was discarded during the subsequent Meiji period and completely ignored after the war.

Now, let us look at their contents. First of all, what kind of ideal leader does this system portray? Someone with "rendered distinguished service, intelligence and thoughtfulness." This is from the opening of the Cannon of Yao in The Classic of History, plainly describing the qualities of an ideal leader. A leader needs to have high military honors or distinguished political success, and has to be very distinct. Since a leader has to solve various problems, he or she has to be equipped with competence, strength and technique. But having these qualities is not enough to be a true leader. A leader also needs to be full of compassion. A leader has to have a desire to understand the views and feeling of others. It also includes a mind which contains the core of the Confucian ideals of jin, or benevolence (affection to wish for others' happiness), and chujo (a sincere and caring heart). Today, we would call it "toughness and kindness." A leader is someone who is equipped with these seemingly opposite qualities.

Another necessary quality is an understanding of the Tao. A leader has to have full understanding of the way of virtue. Although virtue is often interpreted as morality and only the ethical aspect becomes emphasized, it has a lot more substance. It also represents dynamic and energetic creative acts. The Chinese character for "virtue," the core principle of the Chinese classics, used to be pronounced "force," defining the role of leader, supplying the universe's abundant energy to the lives of its people to protect them from illness, calamity and starvation. Also, a person of virtue makes the motto, "give the others one's absolute best," a personal mission. It is someone who earnestly devotes oneself to others or to public welfare, based on this ideal.

How, then, did this system help cultivate such a leader? First, it redefined the definition of "learning." The purpose of learning is, it says, to "seek the nature of true virtue." In short, it is to acquire the virtue previously mentioned. In order to do so, one has to begin with "shu-ko-chi-jin," or governing the nation through cultivation of one's own mind and the accumulation of virtue. A leader has to be able to control the self; otherwise he or she cannot rule others.

What becomes important then is "kokki-fukurei." It means to renounce worldly desires by conforming to one's conscience and reason and return to a harmonious mind. One has to overcome self-interest and discern the essence of common courtesy which is the basis of social order. During the Edo period, achieving "kokki-fukurei" before celebrating one's coming-of-age, fifteen to sixteen years old at that time, was a part of the educational requirements. Children read all four books from the Four Books and Five Classics in order: Great Learning, The Analects, Mencius and Doctrine of the Mean.

The core of what we can learn from the four books is "human nature" and "sociality." The point here is to always "return to one's mind." Successfully governing a nation to sustain peace or having a political ambition to serve the public is important. But, a leader needs to be able to consciously come back to his or her self. This is because having the reins of reform in one's hand at all times is believed to be the key to effective politics. Keeping the nation in order begins with an effective government. An effective government begins with keeping one's family in order. For that, one needs to have an orderly mind at first. Whether global or national affairs, they all originate from the self. One can control the self because one already knows how, but dealing with the world or a state does not happen overnight.

The basis of the education system based on the Chinese classics is that it does not lose sight of realistic solutions. As the saying "a company is a reflection of its workers" illustrates, the importance of good human resources has been acknowledged for a long time. How to foster desirable individuals, on the other hand, is still uncertain. Emphasis on the importance of human resources will continue to increase. A company's fate is going to rest on whether it can intentionally cultivate a desirable future leader. Perhaps, it is time for us to revisit Japan's time-tested, traditional education curriculum of leadership development.

## 2-24 THE SYNTHESIS OF EASTERN AND WESTERN WISDOM

As we ponder on what is in these pages, it becomes clear that the Eastern or Japanese way of thinking – what should be the foundation of our thinking – holds the key to the direction for our future – especially now that we have witnessed many instances where the thinking based on Western scientific rationalism has reached its limit. Dualism, for instance, is a clear example of adverse effects resulting from this approach.

Dualism originates in "mind-body dualism" – Descartes' attempt to separate mind and body to better understand human nature. But in recent years, its negative effects have outweighed the positive. Nonetheless, the thought process of dividing a matter into two has become the basis of our thinking. Similarly, such dualistic approaches are very common in today's business practices, dividing sellers and buyers, managers and employees, individuals and organizations, the American way and the Japanese way, the seniority system and the merit system.

Separating yes and no, or for and against is straightforward, and it does help to indicate which side of an issue one stands. However, it feels like we overlook something very important every time we make such a division. Actually, what we are missing is "innovativeness to overcome" – wisdom to create something new that encompasses elements of both sides instead of resorting to the usual division. It is through this wisdom that we can find true innovativeness.

Another problem with dualistic thinking is that at the instant something is divided, the two sides become opposed to each other. In Japan, people often judge others based on their political inclinations – left or right. The thinking behind it is comprehensible, but the concept is just too simplistic and borderline foolish. Because the two sides are in constant opposition, each side invariably endures attacks from the other side. These attacks can turn very aggressive at times. But most of the people on either side are neither a devoted leftist nor a dedicated rightist. They are moderate whose views are rather in the middle of both extremes. Nonetheless, the attitude to support a more unbiased and sensible "centrist ideology" is still lacking in Japan as people continue to make judgments based on the perceived division.

On the contrary, such way of thinking is absent from Classical Chinese philosophy or most of Eastern thought. According to the principles of yin and yang, two opposing sides are considered as parts of the whole, in complement to one another. The mind and body are not regarded as something that can be separated in a straightforward way. And the fact that they are not simply set apart makes them distinctive. According to these principles, completeness is possible because two conflicting and contradictory aspects coexist.

Another adverse effect of Western scientific rationalism is "analytical specialism." Analytical specialism has earned absolute trust of many as a means to seek truth. Basically it attempts to unveil the true nature of a matter by subdividing it into its smaller parts. Today, analysts in general hold a firm position in Japanese society. Yet, their new-found prominence has brought about a negative consequence. It has caused people to lose sight of the whole. In the field of medicine, for instance, it is like having plenty of specialists for each and every organ, but not a single doctor who can properly care for the whole body. Although doctors are supposed to be able to care for the patients' overall health and wellbeing, too much emphasis on analytical specialism could result in a disproportionate number of specialists whose area of expertise is too limited.

Eastern philosophy focuses mainly on the cultivation of our innate abilities, our brilliant wisdom, to intuitively grasp the whole. Recognized for its relevance to a way of life, this approach has nurtured a number of masters and experts. There are thoughts and ideologies that have been cultivated over thousands of years in the East. Now that we see more harm and contradictions with the Western ways when taken in isolation, what we need is to establish is an ultimate way of thinking through marrying the wisdom of the West and the East. Establishing a truly global ideology through the "synthesis of Eastern and Western wisdom" is the most valuable and necessary foundation for all of us in the twenty-first century.

Today, businesses are also confronted with a spate of problems that conventional approaches do not offer sound solutions to. There are four main issues that need fundamental reform. First is the issue of resources – the primary driving force of any business. The core resources of businesses have shifted from quantitative, such as personnel, goods and money, to qualitative, such as knowledge and brand recognition. Consequently, businesses need to transform themselves to fully reflect such changes.

Second is the meaning of work. What we need is work ethics that center on enriching workers' lives. People no longer work solely to earn an income. They are looking to engage in work in ways that they can look back and say their work was truly fulfilling and enriched their life. Actually, nowadays workers are no longer able to produce results that meet companies' expectations unless they engage in their work in this way.

Third is the business model. We are in an era where products do not sell unless customers see true values in them. Therefore, it is very important for businesses to have a sound business model – a system that is best suited for creating values and a structure that ensures these values are offered effectively.

Last is the issue of mandatory retirement. When steady decline in the number of workers is inevitable, there is no reason to let go of skilled and experienced employees companies already have. Fortunately there is an easy fix to this problem: Readjust the higher seniority wages. Businesses are asked to adopt a new employment system that suits the era of an eighty-year lifespan.

In order to respond precisely to the demands of these times, we need to proactively adopt the Eastern way of thinking which focuses on the fundamental principles of human beings. But we need to keep in mind that this is about the "synthesis of Eastern and Western wisdom," not at all about discarding the Western ways. Aggressive approaches that seek to completely replace the Western ideology with beliefs from the East will only make matters worse.

A wide range of technologies and techniques that originated through the scientific advancement in the West are clearly very valuable. What we need to do is to draw the fundamental principles from the ideology of the East and a wealth of leading technologies and techniques from the West, combine them well and employ this new approach to the fullest. Through successful integration of the best of the both worlds, we will find a new way for businesses for the twenty-first century and their infinite possibilities.

# Afterword

I have spent half of my life pondering and debating with many business owners about how their businesses could overcome the really hot issues, the ones that made them sweat blood, that they found themselves in. I was a part of their efforts in finding ways to contain the situation, recovering their businesses to the point where they could start with a clean slate and turning them around to be profitable. Confronted with such difficult undertakings, these business owners were, understandably, desperate and putting their lives on the line. They were on the brink of losing everything – dangerously close to becoming liable for huge debts which would take them a life time to pay off. I was with them feeling the entire weight of their struggles. There were times that I had to raise my voice so loud to calm these owners down that I surprised even myself. And there were times when we moaned together. These were definitely very difficult moments, but rewarding at the same time.

What helped me tremendously in these situations were the Tao Te Ching, which has accompanied me ever since it saved my life, and other books of classical Chinese philosophy. The two seemingly unrelated fields of business management and classical Chinese philosophy have been distilled inside me over the years to the point where they are completely integrated and indistinguishable from one another. It is not for me to know whether it is good or bad. It may sound irresponsible, but I feel that is the only way that I can put it. But I can say that having closely observed some of the highly distressing business situations, which not many people would have a chance to witness, has been a quite valuable experience. And I am grateful for them.

This book is the manifestation of my experiences and thoughts. For me, it turned out to be a quite memorable undertaking.

At Genmyōsō, Yatsugatake

Yoshifumi Taguchi

www.ingramcontent.com/pod-product-compliance
Lightning Source LLC
Chambersburg PA
CBHW050657160426
43194CB00010B/1971